Do Your Kids a Favor... Love Your Spouse

Kendra Smiley

with John Smiley

All Scripture quotations are taken from the *Holy Bible, New International Version*®. NIV®. Copyright © 1973, 1978, 1984 by International Bible Society. Used by permission of Zondervan Publishing House. All rights reserved.

Cover Design: Garborg Design Works, Inc. Savage, Minnesota.
Cover Illustration: Garborg Design Works, Inc.
Interior Design: LeftCoast Design
Editor: Cheryl Dunlop

Library of Congress Cataloging-in-Publication Data

Smiley, Kendra, 1952-
    Do your kids a favor-- : love your spouse.
    p. cm.
    ISBN-13: 978-0-8024-6942-7
    ISBN-10: 0-8024-6942-6
    1. Parents—Religious life. 2. Spouses—Religious life. 3. Parenting—Religious aspects—Christianity. 4. Marriage—Religious aspects—Christianity. I. Title.

BV4529.S479 2008
248.8'45—dc22

                                                                        2007049747

We hope you enjoy this book from Moody Publishers. Our goal is to provide high-quality, thought-provoking books and products that connect truth to your real needs and challenges. For more information on other books and products written and produced from a biblical perspective, go to www.moodypublishers.com or write to:

Moody Publishers
820 N. LaSalle Boulevard
Chicago, IL 60610

1 3 5 7 9 10 8 6 4 2

Printed in the United States of America

Advice is easily dispensed but wisdom is hard to find, particularly when it comes to raising kids. With bookstore shelves lined with mere advice, do yourself a favor and read the wise counsel Kendra and John Smiley have provided in *Do Your Kids a Favor . . . Love Your Spouse*. This thoroughly biblical, intensely practical, and refreshingly honest book, if followed, will make your marriage strong and your kids secure.

> Dr. Michael Rydelnik
> Professor of Jewish Studies
> Moody Bible Institute
> Chicago, IL

I'm so thankful that Kendra has locked on to a key truth that many seem to ignore. When you love your spouse first and foremost, it's amazing how much security that gives to your children. Kendra is never afraid to tell it like it is.

> Anita Lustrea
> Host & Executive Producer
> Midday Connection

A big thumbs-up to the Smileys for writing this book! Yes, we do our children a huge favor when we love our spouses well. We also illustrate for them the incredible love and faithfulness of God. Thank you, John and Kendra for sharing your beautiful marriage with all of us so that we too can provide a rock-solid foundation of love for our children and grandchildren.

> Wayne Rice
> Co-founder of Youth Specialties
> Founder of HomeWord
> Understanding Your Teenager seminars

This is a delightfully encouraging and inspiring book. Live by this advice and your kids will thank you. Kendra and John live what they write about.

> Jim Burns, Ph.D.
> President, HomeWord
> Author of *Creating An Intimate Marriage*
> and *Confident Parenting*

Kendra and John shed light and wisdom intertwined with humor while they describe not only the benefits of loving your spouse but its imperative nature in raising our children and equipping them for life.

> Denise Zook
> Wife of University of Illinois
> Football Coach Ron Zook

I have known Kendra and John for well over twenty years, and they have always been an inspiration to me in so many ways. Their passion for Christ and their desire to share Him with teenagers is compelling. Their marriage and family life has been a great example for me. I am so glad they have decided to share what God has taught them over the years with us. This book is great, full of truths, and can help anyone at any stage in a marriage. Thank you, Kendra, for allowing God to use you and your personal life lessons in such a teachable way for others.

> Elisa Cupples, mother of four;
> married to Brian for eleven

Whether you're a sparky sanguine or perfect melancholy, John and Kendra provide practical advice on everything from personality differences to family traditions. And they carefully handle the delicate issue of unpacking the baggage we all bring into marriage. I highly recommend this book.

> Florence Littauer
> Speaker and Author

Most of us think of doing favors for our friends. But what about doing a favor for your own children? Kendra and John are here to guide you in giving your kids the best possible favor to love your spouse. Drawing from their own unique backgrounds and perspective, they give great guidance to parents. John's wrap-up of each chapter from The Resident Dad's perspective is worth the price of the book. Want the best for your child? Love your spouse!

> Carole Lewis
> First Place 4 Health National Director

There are many books on parenting, but John and Kendra Smiley's *Do Your Kids a Favor . . . Love Your Spouse* is the one you will find yourself buying for couples who need encouragement, practical wisdom, and a healthy perspective from a mom's and a dad's perspective. The stories will grab your heart, but the unique aspect of this book is that male and female hang-ups, priorities, differences, expectations, mistakes, and solutions are woven together in a way that will make your marriage stronger while you learn how to become a better parent. The couples who work through the section at the end of each chapter will find themselves closer than they've ever been before as they discover how to raise kids right.

> Carol Kent
> Speaker and Author, *A New Kind of Normal*

I've been married going on 18 years and it's funny when you find your-self saying, "Yeah . . . that's exactly how it is!" I think this book cuts right to the chase and tells us how it is and how intertwined our relationships are with not only our spouse but with the Lord. And how important is it for our children to have that loving relationship between Mom and Dad? I have a 14-year-old and I know firsthand how his world is anchored in that safety net. Do you have an issue with your husband or wife? Do you feel like he or she doesn't understand? Grab this book and read a few pages . . . your question may just be answered along with several others.

Scott Andresen
Assistant News Director, WICD-TV
Champaign, IL

As parents we do so much to prepare our kids for a successful life . . . from after-school sports activities, to music lessons, to college prep courses while they're still in elementary school! But who would have thought that loving your spouse could have THE MOST significant impact on their lives today and beyond? Well, thank goodness Kendra Smiley did! In a world where the stability and security of family life is no longer the solid foundation kids can build their lives upon, Kendra, along with her husband, John, turn personal stories, spiritual wisdom and down-to-earth humor into practical advice that will transform ANY household. A book no family should be without.

Kelly Morgan
Co-host of *The Harvest Show*,
LeSEA Broadcasting

Every parent needs to read this book! Most of us make the mistake of putting our children before our spouse unaware of the damage it causes in our marriage relationship. In their honest, straightforward, and humor-ous way John and Kendra Smiley share the secret of keeping your mar-riage a priority in the midst of raising a family.

Jill Savage
Executive Director of Hearts at Home and
author of *Is There Really Sex After Kids?*

Whether you want to prepare for family, improve or rebuild your pres-ent family relationships, this book is on target. Kendra and John give you the tools you need to encourage a closeness between you and your spouse that will steady the legs of any family unit!

J. Otis Ledbetter
Senior Pastor, Sonrise Church, Clovis, CA
Co-Founder, Heritage Builders Association

I love reading Kendra's books because they are so practical and simple to apply to my own life. *Do Your Kids a Favor . . .* is no different. Kendra and John did a great job with this book. It was like I was reading a parenting and a marriage book all wrapped into one. I will definitely recommend this one to my friends.

Elizabeth Alt
Wife of Nathan, mother of four
(with one on the way)

I have advised my sons that to be a good father you have to be a better husband. This book clearly demonstrates the need for parents to focus their relationships on God, spouse, and children in that order. If these ideals are adopted by parents, their children would have a better ability to overcome life's challenges.

D.J. Bushue
Husband of Jennifer, father of two sons

Kendra's book was a very practical and encouraging read. As a mother of four young children I was reminded of how important my relationship with my husband is, and encouraged by the practical suggestions that will not only help our marriage and kids now, but will give our kids a head start in their relationships with their spouses and children in the future. A great book for those with children and those planning on having children!

Mindy LaBerge
Wife and mother of four

"I love this message! Parents can sometimes feel guilty for taking the time to be a couple within marriage. DYKAF is like spending time with a wise friend of long-standing—satisfying, helpful and fun! A blessing for blended families like mine, with solid support for putting your marriage first to the benefit of your children. Sound advice and strong direction for couples who desire a more loving, parent-led family life."

Kim Jeffries
Host, *Along the Way,* Faith Radio Network

This book is dedicated to you, the reader.

*What a blessing it is to know you desire to
#1 Do Your Kids a Favor and
#2 Love Your Spouse.*

*Our prayer is that this book will
help you on that journey.*

Contents

Foreword
11

Introduction
Here Comes the Bride
13

1. Priorities:
First Things First
17

2. Gender Differences:
Men and Women Are Different. Boy, Are They Different!
37

3. Personality Differences:
Why Did I Marry Someone So Strange?
57

4. Unpacking the Baggage:
What Did I Pack Besides Lingerie?
75

5. Family Traditions:
You Call THAT Normal?
91

6. Identity Theft:
Can Someone Really Steal It?
103

Conclusion:
The Fifteen-Year Plan
115

Appendix:
God's Plan of Salvation
117

Acknowledgments
119

Foreword

In thirty-five years of counseling, I have continually observed that a healthy, God-honoring union between husband and wife is at the heart of a loving family. Simply put, children of all ages thrive when they have the security of knowing Mom and Dad are "in it for the long haul."

Unfortunately, many couples today have not been blessed with a model, let alone a blueprint, for building a solid marriage. This is where Kendra and John Smiley come in. Kendra's down-to-earth, honest, often humorous counsel is right on target. The issues she identifies—dealing with your past, setting wise priorities, coming to terms with personality differences between spouses—are ones I have repeatedly seen in my years of listening to couples.

Many young couples today desperately need seasoned marriage mentors who have "been there" to help them along the way. In *Do Your Kids a Favor . . . Love Your Spouse*, Kendra and John Smiley provide just that wisdom.

Gary Chapman
Author, *The Five Love Languages*
and *The Five Languages of Apology*

Here Comes the Bride

"Do you, John, take Kendra to be your wife, to have and to hold from this day forward, for better, for worse, for richer, for poorer, in sickness and in health, to love and to cherish, until death do you part?"

"I do."

"Do you, Kendra, take John to be your husband, to have and to hold from this day forward, for better, for worse, for richer, for poorer, in sickness and in health, to love and to cherish, until death do you part?"

"I do."

"I now pronounce you man and wife. John, you may kiss the bride."

Close your eyes for just a minute and picture the kiss. Hear the traditional bridal recessional as it fills the sanctuary. Imagine me, Kendra, the radiant bride in a flowing white dress standing beside my handsome husband. We turn toward the congregation of family and friends who are smiling delightedly, a few even brushing away a tear or two of joy as the organ plays the triumphant and awe-inspiring recessional. (End of scene 1.)

Now fast-forward to the first conflict between us, the newlyweds.

> "For this reason a man will leave his father and mother and be united to his wife, and the two will become one flesh. So they are no longer two, but one."
>
> (MARK 10:7–8)

Stop! Don't hold that fast-forward button down too long. It was not weeks later or days later or even hours later. The first clash occurred after we had turned and taken three steps back down the aisle.

What, you may ask, could have possibly caused this quarrel? To help you understand, let me describe my bridal veil. It was a full-length veil that trailed elegantly behind me and was attached to a small hat perched on top of my head. The hat was secured to my hair, and I suspect to my scalp, with bobby pins—many, many bobby pins. Conservatively speaking I would guess that there were between two and three dozen of them doing the job. This was *not* an ideal situation. Just dragging the veil behind me was cause for concern for both my veil and my head of hair.

After the pastor pronounced us husband and wife, we turned to march to the back of the church. Before we gained much speed, John inadvertently stepped on my veil. The forward progress of my veil ceased immediately and my entire head jerked backward. The bobby pins held their ground (for better or worse), but I had an instant headache. Knowing that John was unaware of the pain he had just inflicted on his new bride, I smiled bravely and said in a tense, pain-induced whisper, "Don't step on my veil again. That really hurt."

It could not have been more than another two steps before he unknowingly repeated the pain-producing act. My head jerked back once again, and in a quiet but much sterner tone, still smiling for the crowd, I simply said, "If you do that again, I'm going to have to kill you!" I am almost sure that at that moment he (1) still had no idea what he had done and (2) wondered if he had made a big mistake in the marriage!

John was oblivious, to say the least. His mind was not on my veil. In fact, in one of the informal photographs taken as we walked back down the aisle of the church, his attitude was captured exactly. He was pointing with glee at one of his college roommates. His look said it all: "I've done it! I'm married. She's crazy about me. I've survived the wedding, and now it's a quick appearance at the reception and we're off to the honeymoon. I am one excited young man!"

Veil, what veil? Hat, what hat? Bobby pins and headaches, scalp injuries—what did any of those things have to do with the honeymoon? He was ready to get to the "good part."

I don't remember how we resolved our first conflict, but we must have. Since we have now celebrated more than thirty years of marriage, you know the answer to the Dr. Phil question, "Can this marriage be saved?" It obviously was saved, but not without some work.

The recessional ruckus was the first of many beautiful (well, at least "colorful") illustrations of the fact that John and I are different in many ways, including gender. I was wrapped up in the wedding and wanting to be beautiful rather than bald. He was all about the honeymoon and . . . well, you know. What a guy!

The fact that we are different is not bad. It is actually very good. We don't differ on our core beliefs. But in the areas of personality, "baggage," traditions, and, obviously, gender, we are not the same. Our differences mean that we brought differing strengths, talents, experiences, and understanding to our future family. One of us wasn't better or worse than the other; we simply were and are different.

It was our responsibility and privilege to learn to capitalize on the positive attributes of our differences. Why? Quite simply, as a favor to our children. We had to learn to love and appreciate each other as each of us learned about his or her self and about his or her spouse.

You as Mom and Dad each contribute to your family in a unique way. In order to parent successfully, you will need to identify and understand *your* differences and encourage each other as you strengthen your assets—teaching and guiding your children in those positive attributes. Then your kids will:

- Understand gender and personality differences and positively apply that understanding to current and future relationships.
- See the benefit of identifying and dealing with unwanted "baggage" in order to stop its carryover to the next generation.
- Enjoy their family traditions while realizing that other traditions are equally valid.
- Secure their identity in Christ.
- Respect and appreciate the institution, the gift, of marriage and be better prepared to do *their* kids a favor.

On the day of our wedding John and I officially and legally became husband and wife. In a few years, we would become Mom and Dad. We were and are very different. The good news is that we learned to celebrate and capitalize on our differences, and you can too! The differences bring richness to your parenting. They do not have to keep you from working together to raise great kids.

On more than one occasion my brother has reminded us, "Both of you together are much smarter than either one of you alone." It takes all the wisdom both of you, as Mom and Dad, can muster—really the wisdom of God—to raise great kids . . . kids who love God, obey God, and glorify Him with their lives.

Join us as we examine the differences between Mom and Dad—gender, personality, "baggage," traditions, and identity—and how those differences affect parenting. Don't be afraid to honestly evaluate yourself and your relationship. Let us help you identify your strengths and use your differences in practical ways so you will be working *together* to raise great kids. You can do it with God's help. And that is good news, because your kids are counting on you.

CHAPTER ONE

Priorities:
First Things First

Parenting: the toughest job you'll ever love. The task of hands-on parenting lasts for approximately eighteen years, at which point you move from the role of supervisor to that of consultant. Oh, you are always Mom or Dad, but you are no longer involved in daily parenting tasks. And I probably should tell you that, although you are a consultant, you will not be getting paid like one. The shift in responsibilities comes little by little, moving toward the goal of working yourself out of a job.

Many of the choices you make in the early years of parenting have lasting effects. The investment of time and energy that you make in your child can bring both of you joy or sorrow well into the future! Eighteen years may end the parenting responsibilities, but not the relationship.

Let's Make a Plan

With a task this important, a good plan is in order. We all want to know where to go and how to get there. Let's start at the beginning—not by looking at our differences as Mom and Dad, but by examining the things we have in common, our core beliefs.

> "Those who plan what is good find love and faithfulness."
>
> (PROVERBS 14:22)

It is true that my husband, John, and I are very different—different genders, different personalities, different "baggage," different traditions —but despite all of those things, we have the most important fundamentals in common. Our core beliefs are the same. First and foremost, both of us have come to a saving knowledge of Christ . . . at different times and in different ways (of course!), but both of us have arrived at the foot of the cross.

John's Journey

John's journey began at an early age. From infancy through high school he faithfully attended Sunday school and church with his family, hardly ever missing a Sunday. Perfect attendance, however, while admirable, is not a guarantee of a relationship with Christ. That important commitment came when John was sixteen years old. An evangelist was speaking at the little church where John and his family attended, and on the last night of the revival, John went forward to the altar and prayed for forgiveness. That night his heart was changed and he began to seek the Lord and what God had for him.

I think it's safe to say that although that particular evening was monumental for the church, as many people did precisely what John had done, there was no one to disciple and teach those who had made this recent and life-changing decision. So John headed forward on his journey of life knowing that God loved him and that he had been given the gift of eternal life, but knowing very little about the Word of God.

My journey looked nothing like his.

Kendra's Commitment

A few years passed and I came on the scene. We met at the public swimming pool in the town where I lived. I was enrolled in senior life-saving and John accompanied his older brother, our instructor, to help with the final test. He came to the pool on the day that we were scheduled to "rescue the victim!" When I saw how cute he was, I immediately made the decision to get into *his* line. When I saw that all the other girls had the same idea, I simply got into his line first.

I was immediately infatuated with John. The afternoon after our somewhat unusual introduction, I actually told my best friend, Jane, that I thought I had just met the man I would someday marry. Now remember, this was *not* a prophetic statement. This was not based on anything but my human attraction for him. I had done no praying or seeking God's will on the matter, because neither of those behaviors was a part of my life at that time.

We began to date, unaware that the Bible specifically instructs believers (John, in this case) not to be "unequally yoked" with an unbeliever. He was not being overtly disobedient. Instead he was simply oblivious to the instruction of God. After four years, the innocent prediction I had made to Jane came to pass and we were married. We became "yoked"—unequally. John had made a commitment to Christ. I had not. I am certain the inequality contributed to that nasty little interchange I told about in the introduction, which happened shortly after we became husband and wife.

But things did change, and the change occurred soon after our wedding day. John was scheduled to report for pilot training at Big Spring Air Force Base, Texas, about a week after we were married. So we had that honeymoon John had been looking forward to and then we drove to Texas.

I can still remember John waking me up when we got to Texarkana. "Kendra," he said. "We're in Texas now. You might want to stay awake." In our excitement we failed to realize that arriving in Texarkana, more than nine hours into our journey, meant that we were *almost* halfway to Big Spring. Texas is a very large state!

Life in Texas

Ultimately we did reach the Air Force base and John began the adventure of pilot training for the United States Air Force. We got married after I completed my second year of college, so the plan was for me to enroll in college wherever we were stationed. The plan, however, did not come to pass. Big Spring was one of the few bases with no four-year college close by. That seemed to ruin my plans. John's response was that he knew we were "where God wanted us to be."

My thoughts were not as faith-filled. *God? Why does He care where we are stationed? And if He did really care, why didn't He put us near a college?* It didn't make any sense to me. Of course it didn't. "For the message of the cross is foolishness to those who are perishing" (1 Cor. 1:18).

Our different perspectives on location were just one example of how my unbelieving heart was different from John's believing heart. The illustrations mounted daily until finally I became overwhelmed. John's behavior was driving me crazy. He wasn't doing things the way I thought he should. Instead he was at peace in the various challenges. His "annoying" behavior is specifically noted in Scripture. Galatians 5:22–23 says, "But the fruit of the Spirit is love, joy, peace, patience, kindness, goodness, faithfulness, gentleness and self-control." That's how he was responding, and I finally confronted him about it.

"I don't know why you are so content and I am so miserable . . ." I began. Before I could continue, he interrupted me with a thought.

"It just might be that I have accepted Christ as my Savior and I'm not sure you have done that," he said gently.

Just *might?* Not *sure?* There was that kindness and gentleness thing again. He must have known.

But I truly wanted to hear and embrace the Good News of Jesus. I had been seeking the truth since I was a teenager, but had never heard it from someone I knew, loved, and trusted. John was the perfect person to share the gospel with me. He had been "encouraging and comforting" me (1 Thess. 2:12) for several years and now was well qualified to "urge me" just as the Scripture instructs.

"Well, let's get on with it!" I said emphatically. I knew that I wanted what John had. We prayed and my life has never been the same.

I'll be forever grateful . . .

   . . . that we don't have to wait to come to Christ until we are good
      enough.
   . . . that we don't have to wait until we are smart enough.
   . . . that John lived out his love of Christ so that I could see it and
      desire it.

Our core beliefs are the same now, and that is what is most important. We have one other thing we agree completely on (admittedly maybe *only* one other thing). We agree on our list of priorities.

Busy, Busy, Busy

The world is a busy place. Many things clamor for your time and attention. Your kids need you. Your spouse needs you. Your job needs you. Your own parents may need you. And, of course, your church needs you. Just going through that list has worn me out. Everyone needs us. The question is, "What comes first?" That is the age-old question of priorities.

I heard about establishing my priorities when I was in college. I was told that in order to get the most important things accomplished, I'd have to set my priorities. Years later I heard motivational speakers say the same thing. And I read books that encouraged me to make a list of the things I deemed important. All this input had me convinced. *Just do it!* I thought. So I prayed and made a list of the things I thought were important—in order of their importance. I constructed a list of my priorities. This list resided in a place of honor—on the right-hand corner of the desk where I could see it every day. But being able to see my list of priorities didn't change my life. Seeing the list and having it affect my life were two different things.

Motivation for Change

My list of priorities took up space and gathered dust on the corner of my desk until several things happened that motivated me to action. As I spoke around the country, I told anecdotes about my children. In the early years I heard the same comment from more than one older woman. . . . "Oh honey," the woman would say, "enjoy those boys. They'll be gone before you know it!" The recommendation was always expressed with a tone of sadness. I imagined her next words to be "Because, you see, I didn't and now mine are gone! Enjoy those boys. Make them a priority."

Not a bad idea. And something else pushed me in the direction of making my list of priorities actually influence my behavior.

The Oldly-weds

It was a beautiful day in July and a large crowd had gathered to celebrate my in-laws' fortieth wedding anniversary. We had a wonderful

21

dinner and then invited several couples to play the "Oldly-wed Game." The premise of this game was identical to the Newlywed Game with one obvious difference—length of marital commitment. Deep into the competition, the wives had exited the room and the husbands were asked to complete this sentence: "My wife's favorite saying is _____." I'll never forget the answer of one of the contestants. "That's easy," he said. "My wife's favorite saying is 'Hurry up!'" Needless to say, this answer did not match his wife's!

That question and answer from the game got me thinking. How would *my* husband answer that same question? How would my children? "My mom's favorite saying is 'Hurry up!' or 'I'm too busy!'" Yikes! I didn't want either of those sayings to be classified as my favorite or to be featured on my tombstone. My family needed to know by my words and actions that they were a high priority.

Not a bad idea. A good motivator. The most powerful and poignant motivator, however, was yet to come.

No Regrets

One more thing, something much more serious, pushed me to take a long look at implementing the list of priorities into my life. I am the youngest of three children. My brother and sister were both in college by the time I was in third grade. But even with this age gap, my sister and I became friends as adults when we lived within driving distance of each other. My sister's husband, one of my favorite people, was also my dentist.

One day while we were visiting them, he told me he had been having difficulty making extractions. I never realized that it took a certain amount of strength to pull a tooth. Like a typical male, he wasn't even thinking of going to the doctor. Instead he increased his workout schedule. At forty-five years old, he was actually in very good shape. Weeks later, when his aggressive physical fitness plan didn't make a difference, he went to see his doctor.

Immediately the physician declared the problem to be much more serious than anyone realized. My brother-in-law had an MRI and it was determined that he had a brain tumor. Within days he was scheduled for brain surgery.

I was sitting in the ICU waiting room with my sister when the doctor came in after surgery. "We removed some of the tumor from the brain," he said. "We were not able to get the entire mass, however, and it was definitely cancerous. I doubt if he will recover enough to undergo chemotherapy or radiation."

We sat in that waiting room in shock. Over the next few weeks, I went to the hospital to be with my sister and brother-in-law almost every other day. It was more than an hour's drive and I had three young children, but with the help of John's family and our church family, I was able to spend time away.

The conversations with my brother-in-law were difficult. My visits were more of a monologue than a dialogue. I read to him and prayed for him and told him funny stories. My brother-in-law, my sister's husband, my friend, was dying. Because his words were few and far between, they had great impact. One day when I had been in his room for several hours, he turned his head toward me and spoke words I hope I'll never forget. "Oh Sister," he said, "I should have gone fishing more." Those words shouted at me. It was one of the last things he said to me. I needed to consider more seriously my list of priorities.

Not a bad idea!

His words, and his death only days later, were a reminder to me that my list was doing me no good perched on the corner of my desk. It was high time to put that list into action to change my behavior. I wanted to be certain to "enjoy those boys!" I wanted my legacy to be more than efficiency, multitasking, and being in a hurry. And I wanted to be certain I had done what was important in my short time on earth. I didn't want to voice any dying regrets.

So I began more earnestly to pursue the answer to the priority puzzle: How can my "list" be reflected in my life?

Not long after that, I had a thought while I was cleaning the bathtub . . . a job that takes very little attention to detail. I had been thinking about the whole idea of my list of priorities making a difference. I'm pretty sure that the idea was from God because it lined up with His Word and was bigger than any thought I could have had on my own.

My Watercolor Priorities

I had always made my list of priorities on paper with pen or pencil. My idea was this . . . what if I took my paper and put it upright on an easel? And what if instead of a pen or pencil, I painted my priorities with watercolor?

Those of you familiar with watercolor painting are shaking your heads. "This won't work. Watercolor paint will run. You've got to have the paper flat." You're right—right at least about the fact that the watercolors will run to the bottom of the paper. But that was the whole point of the thought I had that day.

Picture this. Priority #1, "The Lord," was written in purple at the top of the sheet of paper. No sooner had my brush left the paper than the dripping paint from the letters I had written began their slow and steady descent to the bottom.

Then I painted Priority #2, "John," my husband. His color was orange. Now orange paint was also running down the sheet . . . blending into the purple from above.

Next came Priority #3, "The Boys." Their color was blue. The blue's downward flow was colored by the purple and orange previously painted.

The same was true with Priority #4, "My Work," painted in green.

And Priority #5, "Other Good Things," was done in red.

The paper I saw in my mind that day was both messy and beautiful. The colors had all raced to the bottom of the sheet. All the words I had written were touched by the paint from words above them on the list. Each thing on my list of priorities was colored or influenced by the things with a higher ranking. My decisions about my work had to be made by considering the *more* important, higher ranking things in my life—the things above it. So, how did I come up with the order on my list? I found this ranking in the Word of God.

The Top Priority

One of my sons was doing a survey for his high school Fellowship of Christian Athletes group. He asked me, "Mom, why do you obey God?"

I answered without hesitation, "Because I love Him."

"Oh, come on, Mom," he retorted. "That's what you're supposed to say. Why do you really obey Him?"

My answer remained the same although I added that initially in my relationship with the Lord, my obedience was probably prompted as much as or more by fear than anything else. As that relationship grew, the motivation was largely love.

The Lord is number one on the chart. God deserves and desires to be first. Recently a friend was telling me his reasoning for following the commands of God. "That is a way we can please God," he commented.

I agreed wholeheartedly, but challenged him with this question, "Why would we want to please Him?" I was prepared not just with a question but with an answer. Continuing I added, "I believe we want to please God when we truly fear Him and love Him."

Scripture has many texts on this subject.

Jesus replied: "'Love the Lord your God with all your heart and with all your soul and with all your mind'" (Matt. 22:37).

"The fear of the Lord is the beginning of wisdom" (Prov. 9:10).

"I, the Lord your God, am a jealous God" (Exod. 20:5).

"You shall have no other gods before me" (Exod. 20:3).

Meeting the Goal

Let's examine what it looks like to have the Lord as your number one priority. It is not a list of do's and don'ts; it is getting to know God. It means investing time in your relationship with the Lord. One very practical way you can do that is by attending worship and becoming involved in a small group where Christian growth is emphasized.

In addition to regular involvement with your church community, it is also important to spend time by yourself in prayer and Bible reading. It might be helpful to check out your local Christian bookstore for a devotional to guide you along the way. I like to read small segments of the Word and really focus on applying the truth in those verses to my life.

The key is to always keep your goal in mind. Your goal is to build on your relationship with the Lord, not to check a square and say, "Good, I've gone to church. I'm all set for another week," or "I just read one chapter in the Old Testament and one in the New, so I can get on with my day." That is not the idea. If you read one verse, only one, and pray that God will teach you about Himself through that verse, you are closer to your goal of building and nurturing a life-changing relationship with your heavenly Father, number one on your list of priorities.

Starting the day in prayer and Bible reading is a good idea. "Very early in the morning, while it was still dark, Jesus got up, left the house and went off to a solitary place, where he prayed" (Mark 1:35). Because the plan is to put God first, it helps to start the morning with our focus on Him. Sometimes we convince ourselves that an hour more in bed is just what we need to start the day out right. I have learned through the years that getting up, getting going, and getting in the Word gives me a better start.

A morning quiet time can set the tone for your day. Your growing relationship with the Lord can then color the decisions of that day. You will become more familiar with His Word and with His nature.

When our kids were young it was more of a challenge to find a quiet time for study and prayer. I convinced myself that I was not created to get up early in the morning. It seemed like I was always one step behind the kids because they started their day before I did. I can still remember telling John that I just couldn't get up early. I was willing to admit that I had trouble getting up, but I was not prepared for his response. "You don't have trouble getting up in the morning; you have trouble going to bed at night." Hmmm . . . a point worth pondering.

Putting your kids to bed on a regular schedule is step one. If they go to bed on or near the same time each night, they will usually be getting up at the same time each morning. Then you can plan your day. Some moms wait until they put their kids to bed and then begin a cleaning frenzy. More often than not, you need to rest and relax more than you need a perfectly clean kitchen floor.

The Hurrier I Go . . .

Just a few months ago I felt more rushed and frenzied than I could ever remember. John and I had been on a teaching/speaking mission trip to Bolivia and our calendar had been jam-packed prior to and after the trip. I am a woman of high energy and I don't like putting things off that, in my opinion, need to be done now. While we were traveling, many such things accumulated. My e-mail inbox was overflowing. I was behind in my self-inflicted writing schedule. Responsibilities at home were piled higher than I could imagine, and I couldn't ignore the duties I had at church.

So I tackled the unbelievable backlog in true Kendra fashion. I determined that all I had to do was work extra-hard and extra-long hours and I would eventually catch up. Unfortunately, my plan did not work. My problem was that I was investing an inordinate amount of time on my number four and five priorities (work and other good things) to the detriment of all the more important things on my list, including number one—the Lord.

One morning as I tried to explain my frustration and stress to John, he stopped me in midsentence. "I just read something that might be of help to you," he said and handed me a book with a chapter on the importance of the Sabbath.

Even though I knew that "remember the Sabbath day by keeping it holy" (Exodus 20:8) was included in the Ten Commandments, I had failed to realize that I was far from being obedient in that area. Sabbath means a time of rest from labor. It occurred to me that I needed to be submissive in this area and take time for silence, solitude, and fasting.

Beginning the very next day, I set aside a morning and let the answering machine take all the messages; let my e-mail go temporarily unanswered; and went to a quiet place (my chair in the family room) with my Bible, a journal, and a copy of *My Utmost for His Highest* by Oswald Chambers.

That morning was amazing! The time of peaceful resting in the Lord was beyond refreshing. It was more than I could have imagined, and I caught a glimpse of why God chose to include a Sabbath rest in His top ten.

Putting the Lord first and building on that relationship is something that will produce many positive results. God's love will become more real. Your ability and desire to love your spouse will grow out of that. Which is, after all, doing your kids a favor!

Number Two

John made it to the number two spot on my list of priorities. Early on it dawned on me that after my relationship with the Lord, my marriage would have the next most longevity. On our wedding day we committed to each other "until death do us part." As the years have passed, my understanding of the covenant we made before God has grown. We may not have initially grasped the extent of the commitment, but it was significant to both of us. God's Word says, "For this reason a man will leave his father and mother and be united to his wife, and they will become one flesh" (Gen. 2:24). I believe that this is not just referring to the physical union of husband and wife, but also a mysterious spiritual connection.

Becoming John's bride has definitely been the second best decision of my life. The first was making a commitment to Christ. You already know that John's actions and decisions drew me to that *most* important commitment. To this day he possesses all of those fruits of the Spirit I told you about earlier—only wavering on occasion. And, if you can believe this, I am still *almost* as infatuated with him as I was the day we met. (If I could bottle that, I'd have a lot of folks clamoring for the concoction!) Furthermore, one of his best attributes is the fact that he is low-maintenance. That is extremely important, because only one high-maintenance adult is allowed per family. ☺

Because John is genuinely pleasant and nondemanding, I want to be sure he realizes his high ranking on my priority list. It is important to know what will communicate my love to him and his importance in my life.

What Time Is It?

John is an "on time" guy. (We'll talk more about that in the chapter on personality differences.) Besides being wired that way, he was a military pilot for thirty years. He synchronized his watch each time he flew.

One way I can let John know that he is important to me is to have meals ready on time. To John that says, "I love you and your wishes are important to me." If you are like me, it says something like, "Oh, is it already time for dinner? OK, I'll be there in just a minute." Timely meals may not be what communicates love to your spouse. But learn how *your* actions can say, "You are important to me—more important than my work or my play—more important than everything and everyone except my Lord."

Give Me a Call

John illustrated my high ranking on his own list by always finding the time to call me no matter where he was in this nation or around the world. The majority of his flying days were before cell phones were in everyone's pocket. He exerted a great deal of energy to reach me by phone almost every day he was gone.

Meals on time (one of John's favorite things), a phone call from John (one of mine), and many other examples told our kids that we placed value in each other and that we considered our marriage relationship to be important. Actually, we were doing the boys a favor. We were loving each other.

The Boys

Third on the list of priorities is our children. Now, most kids could probably understand God coming before them on the list of priorities, but what in the world is Dad doing with such a high ranking? For years I had a cartoon on my refrigerator that illustrated this idea. In the first frame Mom is in her preschool son's bedroom, comforting him as a thunderstorm rages outside. In the next frame, things have calmed down (both inside the house and outside) and the son says to his mother, "Why don't you sleep with me tonight?" Mom replies, "No. I have to sleep with Daddy," and she quietly leaves the room. In the last frame, all alone for the night, the little boy says what is on his mind. "Daddy is such a sissy!"

Kids can be very demanding. Early in their lives they are totally dependent on their parents. That changes as they mature, but leads me to a good point. Ranking does not necessarily indicate time allotment. Instead it indicates influence, with the number one priority coloring decisions about all the priorities beneath it, and so on down the list.

God's Word tells us that children are a blessing from Him. "Sons are a heritage from the Lord, children a reward from him" (Ps. 127:3). They need to be treated as such, but not to come before the higher ranking priorities.

When the boys were little and John would come home from flying for the Air Force Reserves, they would excitedly jump into his arms and want his full attention for as long as possible. Usually after some time spent listening to stories about their day or wrestling with them on the floor, John would announce, "Mom and I are going to talk with each other now," and the boys knew that his undivided attention would now be mine and vice versa.

This acquiescence by our kids to their dad's shift of attention didn't happen by magic. Instead, they had experienced time and time again the undivided attention of their dad and had also seen him show loving attention to me. They had learned the boundaries and that by exhibiting a little patience and allowing the adults to interact with each other, they would soon regain their dad's interest. If this is a pattern you would like to establish in your home, please be patient. It will take awhile for your kids to understand there has been a shift in the priorities. Be consistent. Your kids will learn.

Work

We are down to number four on the list, my work. I love what I do. It is so much fun that on occasion it has drifted upward on my list of priorities. As an author and a speaker, part of what I do entails reading. Ah . . . when engrossed in a great book I can genuinely announce that I am working. And believe me, that is a whole lot more fun than washing the dishes or doing the laundry or even cooking the meals. I used to say that I was a bad cook, but one of my sons pointed out that I was not a "bad" cook. Instead he labeled me a "disinterested" cook. I considered that title an upgrade and am determined to one day write a cookbook for the disinterested cook.

When I first began my home-based business, my husband, John, declared himself my governor. He did not mean "governor" like the esteemed head of one of our fifty states. He was referring to the governor on an automobile—the device that somehow keeps the engine from running too fast. In John's great wisdom, he knew that I needed a little help to keep me (and my Type A behavior) from running too fast. I had to learn how to keep work in its place. God's Word tells us, "Work at it with all your heart, as working for the Lord" (Col. 3:23). It does not say to work constantly. But it is not always easy to keep in check.

The Phone Is Ringing

One of the behaviors that I learned to change to keep my priorities in order was how I handled my business phone calls. There is an amazing phenomenon I have called the "immediate attention response." When your kids are elementary school age, they will be more inclined to tell you about their day if you are available *immediately* when they walk in the door. If I was on the phone, even if I hung up the receiver within minutes of their arrival, it was over . . . I had lost the immediate attention response. Test it out. You will find that it is true. If at all possible, be available the minute you see your kids. Do not be on the cell phone as you pick them up from school or on the phone when they get off the school bus. If you are, you will miss an important time. I learned this, but not as soon as I wish I had.

By the same token, when I was on the phone in the evenings, John felt robbed of time with me. Talking on the phone instead of giving him my attention was not putting first things first. Don't make the mistake I made early on in my business. Keep your priorities in order. Work is number four.

Even Harder for Men

Many times this is even more difficult for men than for women. I hope I never forget a mentoring meeting I had with several young women who were all working in a home-based business. Their biggest concern was that the list of priorities they desired was not the list they were living. Each woman at the meeting listened as I walked the group through the importance of determining priorities and creating a plan to actually live out those priorities.

One woman seemed to be distracted. When I opened the session for questions, this was hers: "How can I get my husband to understand how important we are as his family? He is gone fourteen hours a day and doesn't even connect with the kids on weekends. Last week our two elementary age kids and I vacationed alone in Florida."

This husband had obviously decided that being a provider was more important than investing in his family. The possibility also existed that work was more fun and more rewarding than being a husband and father. The workplace offers accolades and advancement. Most of us do not get promotions, certificates, medals, or raises as we spend time with our family. Those things can seem more important, but they are short-range prizes. A good relationship with your spouse, loving your spouse, has a long-range reward. It is a reward not just for the two of you, but also for your kids.

I asked this woman if she had spoken to her husband about what she was observing—about his choice of work over family. She said she had tried but that he was defensive and did not seem to understand. I suggested that she give her husband the opportunity to learn more the importance of doing his kids a favor by sharing information with him. As wives, one of the least productive things we can do is to badger our husbands or nag about an issue. Sometimes a neutral source like an article from a Christian magazine or a chapter from an inspirational book can become a launching pad for a positive discussion. Both husband and wife are examining what the author is suggesting, and one spouse is not lecturing the other.

She took note of the suggestions and then I simply asked her if she would feel comfortable if I prayed for her situation. Even though it was not a prayer meeting, all those around the table immediately bowed their heads and we joined together in prayer for this hurting wife and mom . . . a woman whose husband did not see the importance of putting first things first . . . yet.

Other Good Things

And last, but not least, we have other good things. This is one category that can really take over your life. "Good things" are making *more* cookies for the "moppets" or being the president of the PTA or chairing the retreat committee or facilitating a small group. All of the tasks noted above are good. And this is the difficulty. We are all too smart to say yes to bad things.

Imagine this conversation . . .

"Kendra, I was wondering if you would have time to do a dastardly deed for me. I've watched you and you're pretty fast on your feet. I think you'd be perfect for the job."

Why, I'd say no immediately, and so would you! We are too wise to sign up for a dastardly deed. But somehow our wisdom takes a vacation when we are asked to do a good thing.

"OK!" "All right." "I guess I could." Those might be the right answers. But sometimes we should say no. The offer must be evaluated in light of our priorities. Does the opportunity measure up when it is colored by the things that have a higher priority, a higher ranking on the list? If we say yes to babysitting our neighbor's kids (a good thing) and spend the next day exhausted and ignoring the needs of our own children, a good thing becomes a bad thing. Have the courage, after considering your priorities, to "Just Say No!" when it is best.

Working Together

This is a book about parenting, about raising great kids. Actually it is a book about working *together* to raise great kids. And who will you be working together with? Your spouse, number two on the list, and the Lord, number one. These relationships are vital because they will color your connection with your kids and greatly shape your ability to raise great kids . . . kids who love God, obey Him, and glorify Him with their lives.

A Good Word from John, the Resident Dad

As a young man recently out of college, I began an exciting adventure. Three days after our honeymoon, Kendra and I packed our bags and headed for Texas, where I was enrolled in pilot training for the United States Air Force. I soon discovered that this training was, in a word, intense. For one year our instructors taught us and trained us and tested us—just to be sure. To be sure that we were capable of flying the aircraft and accomplishing the tasks we were assigned.

Before each training flight my instructor challenged my ability to recite quickly and accurately one or more of the critical emergency procedures. This was part of the preparation. These emergency procedures had to be memorized verbatim. We could not use the manual. We had to know the information perfectly *before* we ever needed to use it. The steps for each procedure had a specific order and the order was extremely important. The priority was crucial. It was often a matter of life or death.

The emergency procedure for "bail out" comes to my mind immediately. It was simple, only two steps. But the order of the steps was vital. #1—Lift handles, #2—Squeeze triggers. Lifting the handles blew the jet's canopy from the aircraft. Squeezing the triggers ejected the pilot's seat from the plane. The importance of the proper sequence, the priority, is very obvious in this example.

Setting priorities and living those out in your daily life is also important. In fact, I believe it is essential for effective parenting. Unlike an emergency procedure in a high speed aircraft, failure to prioritize will probably not cost anyone his life. But our children are depending on us to do the best job we can do. Getting first things first will help you and your spouse work *together* to raise great kids. Maybe you will even be able to avoid some of the unwanted "family emergencies."

John and I Are Just Alike

We . . .

. . . trust in the Lord and strive to put Him first in our lives,
. . . believe in the importance of putting each other next on the list of priorities,
. . . cherish our children and have seen them grow to be responsible adults,
. . . work hard, and
. . . share our time, talents, and gifts with others.

John and I Are Very Different

We are . . .
  . . . a man and a woman,
  . . . an extrovert and an introvert,
  . . . a person who was loaded down with "baggage" and one whose
      bags were light, and
  . . . an individual whose traditions included Sunday school and
      church and one whose did not.

We share the same core values, yet we are as different as night and day.
But we have both chosen to love each other. Let's see how that looks to a
man and to a woman, specifically how it looks to you and your spouse,
because I am sure you already know that men and women are different.

Time for Some Honest Evaluation

1. Describe the events surrounding your decision to accept Jesus
   Christ as your Savior.

2. How has your decision to accept Christ affected your decisions
   and behavior in regard to your priorities?

3. Write down what you *desire* your top five priorities to be.
   (1)
   (2)
   (3)
   (4)
   (5)

4. Write down your current top five priorities, which may not be the
   same as your answer to the last question. That is OK. Be honest.
   (1)
   (2)
   (3)
   (4)
   (5)

5. Where did you rank your spouse on the priority list?

6. Where would your spouse say he or she is ranked?

7. If you have any priorities that you consider out of order, choose one you would like to change.

8. What are some practical steps you can take to get that priority in order?

9. Within the next week, discuss your answers to these questions with your spouse. If there are differences in your priorities, take time to talk about them. Write out a plan of how to "get on the same page" with your top five priorities.

CHAPTER TWO

Gender Differences: Men and Women Are Different. Boy, Are They Different!

The phone rang and I picked it up. "Hello."

"Hi Mom." It was our son Aaron, a freshman in college at the time.

"What's up?" I asked, wondering what had prompted this midday call.

"Not much," he began, and then after a minute or two of chatting he got to the real purpose of his call. "Mom," he said in a more serious tone, "I need you to think like a girl for a minute."

This request caught me by surprise. What did he think I usually did? I guess in his mind I thought "like a mom"—an aging derivative of a girl. I no longer remember the issue we went on to discuss, but evidently I adequately fulfilled his request to "think like a girl." This was important to him because, as a man, he was not capable of the task and, at that point in his life, I was the best resource he had.

Do men and women think differently? Absolutely, positively yes! (I can't even believe I jotted down that question.) The anatomical differences between a man and a woman are the easiest to identify, but they are only one aspect. Even the scientific community has admitted, although reluctantly, that men and women are different. Boy, are we different!

Science to the Rescue

From our gender-based ability
We research the validity
And state with credibility
That men and women differ.

Through the ages, the differences between the genders have been cause for discussion, debate, humor, and even scientific research. In the 1970s the debate was raging about the superiority of one gender over the other. The common theme was that men and women were the same. If there were any differences, many thought, those were a result of nurture not nature.

"Give a little girl a toy truck and a little boy a doll," it was claimed, "and the traditional roles and behaviors would be reversed." The main problem (but not the *only* problem) with the theory was that it was wrong. More typically, rather than reversing roles, a little girl with a toy truck pretended to take her family for a ride. A boy with a doll grunted orders to it as together they prepared for battle against some unnamed foe. Nevertheless, the questions continue. But rather than examine this study or that one, rather than go to the scientific community for answers, let's take a look at what the Bible has to say.

The Bible Tells Me So

God created all humanity.
He knows our capability
To live in the reality
That men and women differ.

Right back at the beginning of time, God made us man and woman.

Then God said, "Let us make man in our image, in our likeness, and let them rule over the fish of the sea and the birds of the air, over the livestock, over all the earth, and over all the creatures that move along the ground." (Gen. 1:26)

The Lord God said, "It is not good for the man to be alone. I will make a helper suitable for him." Now the Lord God had formed out of the ground all the beasts of the field and all the birds of the air. He brought them to the man to see what he would name them; and whatever the man called each living creature, that was its name. So the man gave names to all the livestock, the birds of the air and all the beasts of the field. But for Adam no suitable helper was found. So the Lord God caused the man to fall into a deep sleep; and while he was sleeping, he took one of the man's ribs and closed up the place with flesh. Then the Lord God made a woman from the rib he had taken out of the man, and he brought her to the man. (Gen. 2:18–22)

So God created man in his own image, in the image of God he created him; male and female he created them. (Gen. 1:27)

Both man and woman are created by God and they are distinct in their genders. Men and women are different. After extensive scientific research *Time* and *Life* magazines both reported that fact. It doesn't take research or the skill of a rocket scientist to come up with the truth. It is supported by common sense and, more important, by the Word of God.

The Mouths of Babes

I remember when our oldest son came home from school a little confused. He was ten years old and in the fourth grade.

"Kristen McB. has been acting weird lately," Matthew began. "She's always been my friend, but there's something different about her."

"What do you mean by 'weird' and 'different'?" I asked. "What has she been doing?"

"Well, for one thing, she borrows my pencil and then she won't give it back!"

With that explanation, John joined the conversation. "Matthew, let me see if I can explain it to you. About fourth grade, girls start getting weird and acting a little different. And they get weirder and weirder the older they get. But the amazing thing is that in about five years or so, you'll actually start to enjoy the weirdness and the difference."

That was it. End of conversation. Matthew nodded knowingly and headed out to play. I was not upset and did not feel insulted. I merely sat in amazement at the simple yet relatively accurate explanation given by his father.

The Favors

As we take a look at the gender differences, we will emphasize three favors—three favors that will benefit your child as you love your spouse. Your child will:
1. Feel valued as a boy or girl.
2. Learn to appreciate gender differences.
3. Experience a positive model for marriage and healthy interpersonal relationships.

Let's begin at the beginning. Men and women, boys and girls, are different! Boy, are they different!

No Mistake

Your children need stability,
Your love, dependability,
God's grace, availability
Learning men and women differ.

The amazing truth that men and women are different is not a mistake. God knew what He was doing when He "created man in his own image, in the image of God he created him; male and female he created them" (Gen. 1:27). God was more than aware that the two genders would be distinct and have unique strengths for parenting. It was all a part of the plan. You, as Mom and Dad, are both assigned the task of nurturing, teaching, and lovingly disciplining your children. You each bring definite strengths because of your gender. Your child benefits greatly because you are not the same.

Mother, May I?

I'm guessing you had a pretty good idea as a child which parent to consult when it came time to get permission for an activity perceived as dangerous. The chances are great you asked your father. Usually kids ask Dad if they can do the risky things.

"May I ski down the double black diamond?"

"May I ride the horse bareback?"

"May I skateboard on the vertical ramp?"

You asked your dad because the odds were better that he would say yes. Dads are usually the risk-takers. It's a guy thing. Moms tend to be more protective. It's a woman thing. Trust me, your kids have already figured that out. The ideal situation is to have a balance between danger and protection.

How can this balance be achieved? Talk together, you and your spouse. It is best to have this conversation when it is just the two of you. If you find yourselves at the extremes of the continuum, your goal will be to find a solution that is a compromise by both of you. It will probably be very difficult to arrive at the perfect midpoint. Keep in mind that the balance, in this case between protection and risk, needs to be in the best interest of your child. It is not a competition to see which parent will "win."

Your child needs to be safe but not smothered. Taking a calculated risk, trying something new, stretching (but not breaking)—those are all important parts of growing up. You and your spouse bring different perspectives that will benefit your child. Your job is to find that balance. Then your child will learn that one gender is not better or worse than the other; they are just different.

Protection Overload

I know a little boy who is growing up in a single-parent household. Actually, to be more accurate, he is in a home with three adult women: his mother, his grandmother, and his aunt. He and his father have limited interaction and his grandfather is deceased. As a result, he has only a small amount of male influence with very few opportunities to experience risks and adventure.

This grade school age boy has been subjected to an inordinate amount of protection. Even though the women in his life are loving and kind, he longs for the fun of even simple explorations and excitement. He is prohibited from climbing trees and testing out the playground equipment his caretakers deem dangerous. He has not been encouraged to ride a bike or to wrestle on the floor.

His situation is an example of a lack of balance between the male influence (adventure, danger, and risk) and the female influence (protection). To achieve this balance, the young man would need to interact with positive male influencers, perhaps through an organization like the Cub Scouts or baseball. Mom, Grandma, and Auntie could also help him by realizing the overload of female influence and by making every attempt to be less protective.

Maintaining Balance

Your child may be blessed with a two-parent home, but may still be experiencing an imbalance between protection and risk. If you are over-compensating in either area, you and your spouse need to take a step back and ask, "Why is there an inequity?" Is your child being excessively sheltered because Dad is not playing an active role in his or her daily life? Is she too much of a risk-taker because Mom's influence is somehow being negated? Your son or daughter needs to know that both positions, while potentially "opposite" on the continuum, are legitimate.

The key to finding balance is negotiation. Your kids will learn valuable lessons as they witness give-and-take between the two of you. Being respectful of a different perspective is the key. Avoid condemning your spouse's opinion. Your husband or wife's position is not stupid, ridiculous, or absurd. Instead it is different. Disagreeing in a courteous way is important.

The concept of "politely disagreeing" is lost when either you or your spouse forgets the purpose of the negotiation. You are negotiating for the good of your child. It is not about you. It is about loving your spouse as a favor to your child. That means if you choose to engage in name-calling, you have lost sight of the purpose. It has become all about you, and the next thing you know, you and your spouse will be in a heated discussion about the argument itself and not the original issue. Negotiation is best done with as little emotion as possible.

Your child will discover that there are times when Dad's position is correct. There are times when Mom's position is correct. And there are times when the best answer is right in the middle. Understanding this will validate your child's instincts as a boy or girl and value him or her. Your child will see that both responses can be valid in different situations. You will be moving toward the accomplishment of the first favor. The man or woman your child was created to be is not a mistake, but is, instead, a part of God's loving plan.

In addition, as you and your spouse work together to achieve a balance between the masculinity and femininity represented by each, your child will learn to appreciate gender differences. That is the second goal to be achieved by loving your spouse—the second "favor" you will be doing for your child.

And finally, your son or daughter will witness an example for his or her future role as an adult. Your child will experience a positive model for marriage and healthy interpersonal relationships.

Mom's Forte

Dads may be better able to encourage adventure, but we moms also have our forte. I've already given you one example: "Mom, I need you to think like a girl." For the most part, moms are much better at listening and talking about feelings. We are better because we have been practicing that art for a long time—long before we became moms—since back when we were only "girls."

The Bad Day

Shelby came running out to her mom's car in the school parking lot. "How was your day?" Mom asked.

"Horrible!" she said with great drama. "I forgot that it was band day and I left my flute at home. Mrs. Stevens gave me permission to call you, but the secretary was on the phone *forever* and I finally gave up. I got a check mark from the director. She was really unhappy with me. Then when it was time for spelling, I remembered that I had put my spelling paper in my flute case so I didn't have my homework to hand in. I got an incomplete and had to miss recess. And they were playing four-square today! Lunch was cold meat sandwiches and I hate them. PE was cancelled because by then it was raining, and I have tons of homework! It was *not* a good day!"

Mom spent the next few minutes encouraging and comforting her daughter. By the time she was finished with her "mother's monologue," Shelby had put things back into perspective. She had been convinced that tomorrow would be a better day.

I do not want to suggest that this little girl would not have told her dad about the negative events of the day, but the chances are that she would not have gotten through the entire litany. That is because, as a man, he would have jumped in at the first breath with some possible solutions. It's a guy thing. It's what they do.

"Let's see," he might have said, "what if you set your instrument right by the front door before you go to bed. That way you'll see it and not forget it." Not a bad idea, but this young lady was not looking for solutions when she started the conversation. Dads are great at solutions, not always so good at listening. If at all possible, men want to fix things.

There are times when a solution is desired, but there are times when it would just get in the way. Always fixing things is no more correct than never fixing things. No matter what the natural response of your children, seeing the balance will be important to them. As your children witness the differing responses of Mom and Dad, they will gain confidence in who they are and feel valued as a boy or girl.

As a husband, John had to *learn* that I didn't always want him to fix things. On more than one occasion, I have said, "You don't need to solve this problem. Just listen to me and nod." Often our sons heard me say that too. They learned, as their dad learned, that even though they might be able to come up with the perfect answer to a dilemma, there were times when it was best to keep that response to themselves. Why? Because men and women are different.

As your child witnesses episodes like this, he will discover that it is OK not to fix everything right away. That it is OK to express a need, like the need to be comforted, and to help your loved one understand. That will also help your child learn to appreciate gender differences.

Your children will be listening and watching. At times they will see Dad loving Mom by just listening to her. Other times they will witness Mom loving Dad by asking for possible solutions. In future years they will be able to duplicate those behaviors, those positive models. It is good for them to experience a positive model for marriage and healthy interpersonal relationships.

He Said, She Said

Communication plays an important role in loving your spouse. God communicated His love to us in that "while we were still sinners, Christ died for us" (Rom. 5:8). "For God so loved the world that he gave his one and only Son" (John 3:16). We do things that communicate our love for each other, verbally and nonverbally. As we communicate love to our spouses, we underline their value in our lives. But what about the difficulty men and women have (seemingly by nature) communicating with one another? You know, the old "He said, she said."

Husband says: Did you put garlic on the roast?
Wife hears: I hate your roast. You always put too much garlic on it. I like my mother's roast much better than yours. Maybe you should just stop trying to make a good roast.
Husband means: Did you put garlic on the roast?

Or . . .

Wife says: I hope we have some time to just enjoy each other when we go to bed tonight.
Husband hears: I can hardly wait to jump in the sack with you. You had better get ready for some great sex tonight!
Wife means: If I haven't already fallen asleep by 8:30, I'd really appreciate it if you would rub my feet when we go to bed.

Or . . .

Husband says: I did the dishes while you were at the grocery store.
Wife hears: The table has been cleared off. The dishes and pots and pans are washed and put away. The kitchen is spotless.
Husband means: I've pushed the dirty dishes in the direction of the dishwasher.

Or . . .

Husband says: I took care of my clothes.

Wife hears: My clothes are hung neatly in the closet.
Husband means: My clothes aren't on the floor. They're on a chair.

Or . . .

Wife says: Do you think these pants make me look fat?
Husband hears: It doesn't matter what you say about these pants. I'll
    either call you a liar or simply refuse to speak to you.
Wife means: I'm feeling a little insecure about my figure lately. Oh,
    and good luck answering the question I just asked.

It is essential that you love each other even as you experience those verbal misunderstandings. Be aware that your responses are being monitored by your kids. These are teachable moments for them. When there is confusion, it is no secret that someone is upset. The key to better communication is not necessarily to repeat your words slower and louder. When you realize that there has been a miscommunication, try rephrasing your statement. Being annoyed does not accomplish your goal of loving your spouse, so do not waste time with that. Instead strive to be a better listener by focusing on the conversation. Men, that might mean turning off, turning down, or pressing Pause as you watch TV. Women, that will mean you must stop your multitasking and listen with your ears, your eyes, and your heart.

Men and women hear differently and they speak differently too. Good communication between husband and wife is an art (some might consider it a miracle), but it is possible. Men tend to be more straightforward and direct. Women's communication is usually lengthier, with nuances that are too often missed. As you are able to work through the communication confusion with give-and-take from both Mom and Dad, your son or daughter will learn that even though men and women exchange ideas and transfer information in two very different ways, both of those ways are legitimate.

FYI These examples of gender differences are not absolutes, not 100% guaranteed, and not an example of "thus saith the Lord." ☺

As you respond in love to a miscommunication, and allow your spouse to do the same, your child will learn to appreciate your gender differences. Knowing how to verbally connect with another person is greatly enhanced as the typical gender differences are understood and appreciated.

And finally, whether you are the one who is expressing yourself in a confusing manner or the one who is a poor listener, your responsibility as a parent and a loving spouse is to illustrate a Christlike, mature response to the situation. That will help your child experience a positive model for marriage and healthy interpersonal relationships.

You are teaching your children how to relate to others. You are doing them that favor by loving your spouse.

Living Illustrations

You and your spouse are living illustrations of the differences between men and women. We have already identified that, typically, men are action-oriented and problem-solvers and women are more protective and nurturing. Furthermore, communication between the genders is not always easy. Helping your child feel valued as a boy or girl; teaching him or her to appreciate the gender differences; and modeling a positive marriage relationship and healthy interactions with others are important, affirming lessons. Your home is a learning laboratory for future relationships.

It is inevitable that there will be both "better and worse" between Mom and Dad, and some of the "worse" will undoubtedly be prompted by the gender differences. Let's examine some practical ways you can emphasize the "better" and minimize the "worse" as you do your kids a favor and love your spouse.

Valuing Feelings

There is no doubt in the mind of either men or women that we females have feelings. We are quick to remind our husbands not to forget about our feelings and emotions. "You *never* think about how I feel." "That hurt my feelings." "You're so insensitive."

If you are a wife, it is possible, maybe even probable, that you have not heard those same statements from your husband. Too many times we women are unaware that our husbands possess sensitivity or emotions.

Likewise, men have been conditioned to suppress their feelings and to refrain from expressing them, verbally or nonverbally. In extreme situations, the birth of a child or the death of a loved one, for example, we catch a glimpse of our husband's emotions, but the minor experiences of day-to-day living may elicit few emotional responses.

Because this is typically the case, a woman may have falsely concluded that men have no feelings. That was precisely the case for me, and it is definitely an error in thinking. If you doubt the emphatic conclusion just stated, consider this—God has given men a task involving supreme emotional sensitivity. God has instructed every husband to *love* his wife as Christ loved the church (Eph. 5:25). He didn't tell the husband to *reason* with his wife or to *appease* his wife. He told the husband to *love* his wife. God made men capable of that highly emotional task.

Your husband has feelings. He may not have the words or training to express them, but they still exist. Most likely he has not practiced verbalizing how he feels. He may be able to express what he thinks, but it is a different thing to express how he feels. Women practice the expression of feelings all the time. When we meet with a girlfriend for lunch, we don't necessarily discuss the weather or sports or any other current events; we talk about what is on our hearts. We verbalize our emotions. That is not true for men. They experience joys and hurts and insecurities just as women do, but many times these are never expressed.

As a loving spouse, you need to help your husband identify those feelings and emotions and to express them. Step one in that process is, obviously, to acknowledge that your husband *has* emotions. I can hear some of you right now. "Kendra, you don't know my husband. He does not have any feelings other than anger, which is expressed with gusto when I forget to fill up the car with gas."

You will just have to trust me on this one. Let's consider some helpful hints. Men, these are good for you too as you validate your wife's emotions.

1. Be patient. Be a listener.
2. No nagging. It will not encourage your husband to think about how he feels. It will probably do just the opposite.
3. Don't demand that your spouse "open up and share." It may have to be enough for now that you are aware that somewhere in the dark recesses of his masculinity, he has feelings and emotions.

4. Never ridicule your mate for feelings he or she expresses. Never.
5. When someone chooses to reveal his or her feelings it makes that person very vulnerable. Do not use this intimacy as a weapon.

When your kids, boys or girls, witness the loving freedom that you and your spouse have to discuss your feelings, they will have increased confidence to share theirs. Everyone has emotions, whether those are buried, masked, or freely displayed. Being a young man with feelings is OK. Being a young woman with feelings is OK too. Being able to express emotions does not indicate superiority. Neither does being able to suppress them.

I was raised in a home where the adults didn't always speak in a loving way with one another about emotional matters. More often, it was a shouting match followed by displays of anger and crying. The expression of the negative, hurtful emotions that I witnessed as a child is much different from the positive, constructive sharing of emotions that I am suggesting. When you as Mom and Dad convey your feelings in a constructive way, your children will experience a positive model for marriage and healthy interpersonal relationships.

Second Best?

Too often, one gender is valued over the other. A man was present at the birth of his second daughter. As this precious young thing took her first breath, her father lamented, "Well, we got second best again." Sounds awful, doesn't it? Unfortunately that idea is in the back of some minds even if they are too smart to put the idea into words. I believe it will be difficult for this man's daughters to realize their value unless he has a change of attitude.

Years ago I saw a plaque on the desk of a woman in leadership. The quote said, "God created man. Then he created woman and finally got it right!" No. God created man and woman and He "got it right" both times. No daughter or son is "second best." Each is the child God has chosen for your family. Each child is of great worth to the Lord. It is up to you and your spouse to be certain that you are communicating that truth in your words and your actions.

How do you see to it that your child feels valued as a boy or girl and is learning to appreciate gender differences? First you must evaluate your own thoughts and feelings about both genders. Maybe you were raised to believe that one gender was superior.

Perhaps it is difficult for you to personally accept God's love as a man or as a woman. Your primary assignment is to deal with any teaching from your past that is contrary to the truth of God's Word (Galatians 3:28 says, "There is neither Jew nor Greek, slave nor free, male nor female, for you are all one in Christ Jesus"). Eliminating this sort of baggage could be a difficult task, but it will benefit you, your spouse, and your kids. Remember our first goal is that your child will feel valued as a boy or girl.

Your children need to understand their value in God's eyes, and a great deal of that is how they perceive your and your spouse's opinions of each other as man and woman. They are watching you and drawing conclusions about their worth and the worth of their genders based on what they see and hear from you.

After you unpack some of the inaccurate, damaging baggage, it is time to evaluate your verbal and nonverbal communication with your spouse. The wife or husband who belittles a spouse is not communicating love, respect, or the value of that individual. That sort of behavior is not advancing our second goal: that your child will learn to appreciate gender differences.

It is unfortunate that men and women are typically misrepresented in the media today. In the name of humor, dads are seen as misfits, inept, and incapable of being husbands or fathers. I cringe when I see those sorts of portrayals or when I hear women demeaning their husbands.

I feel the same way when that attitude comes from the lips of husbands and fathers or from the media. Moms are portrayed as domineering and heartless or as complete morons. These images are broadcast daily to our children. Mom and Dad, you will have to work hard to counteract this cultural influence. You can do it with God's help. Instead of making light of the differences between man and woman, encourage your child to see the value of husband and wife from God's perspective. Value your spouse. Then your child will experience a positive model for marriage and healthy interpersonal relationships.

Dad, compliment your wife on her ability to make your house a home, a place of refuge for the family. Mom, thank Dad for working hard and providing for the family. Make a list of some of your husband's specific traits that you appreciate, and look for ways to communicate your appreciation. Dad, you do the same. Your kids are being encouraged and validated as future men or women, husbands or wives by witnessing a positive model of marriage.

Abuse

Undoubtedly, the most demeaning and disrespectful thing a man or woman can experience is abuse. I was listening to an interview with a woman who had been abused by her husband. It was quite moving throughout, but in my mind nothing compared to one of the last statements the woman made. The interviewer asked if her husband had ever abused their children.

"When a man abuses his wife, he is automatically abusing their children," was her straightforward answer. The point was clear. Failing to love your spouse has a very negative effect on the children. Anytime a spouse is treated with contempt, the entire family is wounded. Avoid that negative behavior.

Personal Experience

I am the adult child of an alcoholic. I grew up in a dysfunctional home and had a distorted view of several things. My parents showed little respect or love to each other. As a result, I doubted their love for me and my worth and value as a young woman. My recollection is that in our home I was never told of God's love or of His caring and love for me personally. Those omissions led to some serious insecurities.

The adults did not do a good job of teaching me that men and women think and respond differently. I was not aware that this was natural and to be appreciated. Consequently, I did not imagine that my point of view or innate ways of responding were of value. And, similarly, I did not gain a positive model for marriage and healthy interpersonal interactions.

But before I continue on this downward spiral, let me remind you of one of the positive things we can model and teach our children regardless of our own situations. It is this: You are responsible for how you respond to your circumstances, whether or not you have any control over them. In my case, I did not have control of my father's alcoholism. However, through the grace of God, He revealed to me that my responsibility in the circumstances was to choose my response.

My passion for parenting stems in a large part from my turbulent experiences as a child. I was on the receiving end of some poor parenting. I am not suggesting that you create that passion for parenting in the same negative way. Instead give your kids a model worth emulating.

A Work in Progress

I am a work in progress. Do I find that a depressing admission? Yes and no. It would be nice to be able to say that I had arrived (although I wouldn't be fooling anyone!). The truth is that none of us has "arrived" at this point. The good news is probably the words "in progress." As long as I am experiencing forward motion . . . as long as I am not complacent in my learning and growing, that is positive.

Marriage should be a duet——when one sings, the other claps.
JOE MURRAY

My desire is to become a more loving wife even though our children are no longer living under our roof. Our sons all have wives, their own very special, very different people to love and cherish. I know, however, that our influence as Mom and Dad never stops. It has been greatly diminished from the days of hands-on parenting, but we still have the privilege and the responsibility of being a part of their lives.

Chances are you are in the thick of things when it comes to parenting. Or maybe you are contemplating the adventure and getting a jump start by reading this book. This is a precious time in your life . . . to be followed by many more. Start today. Do your kids a favor. Love your spouse.

Aaron's Call——Take Two

Remember the phone call with which we began this chapter, when my son Aaron told me, "I need you to think like a girl for a minute"?

The truth is I always think like a girl, a woman, and John always thinks like a man. Our task as parents is to do our best to understand and accept the gender differences, work together, and appreciate those differences. That is your responsibility too. When you do that, your kids are the big winners. They will learn to feel confident in who they are as individuals, appreciating the strengths of men and women—future husbands and wives—future dads and moms. Do your kids a favor. Love your spouse.

> From our gender-based ability
> We research the validity
> And state with credibility
> That men and women differ.
>
> God created all humanity.
> He knows our capability
> To live in the reality
> That men and women differ.
>
> Your children need stability,
> Your love, dependability,
> God's grace, availability
> Learning men and women differ.
>
> God created all humanity.
> He knows our capability
> To *treasure* the reality
> That men and women differ!

A Good Word from John, the Resident Dad

God gave me a very clear picture a few years ago of how important it was for me, Dad, to love Kendra, Mom. I was reading in Proverbs 30. I came to verse 21, "Under three things the earth trembles, under four it cannot bear up." Even though I had read that verse several times before, I had never given much thought to the "list" that appeared in the following verses. Verses 22–23 give the list: "a servant who becomes king, a fool who is full of food, an unloved woman who is married, and a maidservant who displaces her mistress." I was startled and reread the third item again . . . "an unloved woman who is married." A husband failing to love his wife makes the earth tremble.

I have never experienced an earthquake, but I can imagine what it must be like to feel the earth moving and shaking violently. Think about the fear on the faces of individuals who are experiencing the movement under their feet. That is precisely what happens when a wife is not loved by her husband. There is no stability. Things shake and fall, crack and break. Destruction is rampant and the children are in the epicenter of the devastation.

Your children are affected greatly when Dad does not love Mom. They are living in an earthquake zone. Their home is trembling. Will their family be completely destroyed? The answer is unclear, but we are certain that "the earth trembles because of an unloved married woman."

Do your kids a favor. Love your spouse.

More than Gender Differences

It isn't just the gender differences. More times than not, the extrovert is attracted to the introvert. The joker falls in love with the straight man. The hard-charger is fascinated by the relaxed one, and the list-maker marries the scatterbrain. Then each spouse asks, "Why did I marry someone so strange?" Read on. Opposites have a great deal to teach their kids as they love one another.

Time for Some Honest Evaluation

1. Mark your position on the following continuums.

Protector _____ Risk-taker

Nurturer _____ Problem-solver

Now mark your estimate of your spouse's position. Ask your spouse to do the same and see how your evaluations compare.

2. He said . . . She said. Think of the last time when you and your spouse experienced a miscommunication. How was it resolved? If your kids were aware of the problem, did they also witness the resolution? That can provide an important teachable moment.

3. Biases from your youth can influence how you view the worth of each of the genders. As you reflect on the influence of your own parents, do any of those biases come to mind? Do you believe that might be a factor for your spouse?

4. Name one way you purposefully affirm your spouse in his or her gender difference. What does your spouse do to affirm you as a man or woman?

5. If it is true that your home is a "learning laboratory" for your kids, what lessons have they been learning about the differences between and the value of men and women? What lesson would you like them to learn?

6. Men and women both have feelings. Five helpful hints were given to aid you in assisting your spouse in identifying his or her feelings and emotions and expressing them.

   Number 1—Be patient! Be a listener.
   Number 2—No nagging.
   Number 3—Don't demand that your spouse "open up and share."
   Number 4—Never ridicule your mate for feelings he or she expresses.
   Number 5—Do not use the intimacy of revealed feelings as a weapon.

Which number speaks the loudest to you? Which one do you hope your spouse will take to heart?

CHAPTER THREE

Personality Differences: Why Did I Marry Someone So Strange?

When I was in my teenage years, the *Reader's Digest* featured some sort of personality test in almost every other issue. I found those tests fascinating and eagerly completed every one I encountered. Interestingly enough, I always filled in the answers with pencil. I never used a pen. That was a calculated decision. After all, what if the test showed that I had a bad personality? I didn't want anyone else to discover that!

You know as well as I do that personality tests do not indicate whether you have a good or bad personality. Instead the idea is that the test results will help you understand yourself better.

Understanding yourself may or may not be an easy job, but understanding your spouse is almost always complicated! I believe that is true because, in many cases, opposites really do attract.

The extrovert admires the strong, silent nature of the introvert. The introvert is fascinated by the outgoing, never-met-a-stranger extrovert. The scatterbrain is longing for a relationship with an organized planner and list-maker. The individual who lives by charts and graphs likes the spontaneity of Mr. or Miss Life of the Party. These opposites meet, fall in love, and marry—attracted to each other because of the strengths—so different from their own. Then, ultimately, comes the question, "Why did I marry someone so strange?"

Maybe you have asked that very question. Maybe your spouse has too.

You married that amazing man or woman because of the strengths in his or her personality, and then the assignment became how to live with the weaknesses. That is all a part of doing your kids a favor and loving your spouse. The fact that you are not the same, though challenging, is very good for your children. Opposites have a great deal to teach their kids as they love each other.

Understanding Your Temperament

Even though I took all those *Reader's Digest* tests as a teen, it was much later that I discovered there were labels and categories for the various personalities. I learned that defining the temperaments went beyond the main divisions of extrovert and introvert.

My introduction to the art of understanding the temperaments came when my friend Shirley insisted that I read the book *Personality Plus* by Florence Littauer. Shirley guaranteed me that not only would I enjoy it, but I would also learn something in the process. And she was correct. Littauer, influenced in her writing by Dr. Tim LaHaye's *Spirit-Controlled Temperament*, did an amazing job of making each personality type come alive. She also has an inventory at the end of the book so that the reader could determine his or her personality.

Go to http://lynn_meade.tripod.com/id139.htm to take the test yourself.

The popular sanguine is an extrovert, a talker, friendly, and cheerful. Also an extrovert, the powerful choleric is a born leader and a confident, take-charge person. These two are natural blends and categories where I score the highest.

The perfect melancholy is a thinker, detail conscious, and genius prone. The natural blend with a melancholy is a peaceful phlegmatic, an easygoing person who is an excellent mediator. These two personalities belong to John.

What's Your Type?

THE POPULAR SANGUINE—
The Extrovert, The Talker, The Optimist

STRENGTHS	WEAKNESSES
Emotions	*Emotions*
Appealing personality	Compulsive talker
Talkative	Exaggerates and elaborates
Good sense of humor	Dwells on trivia
Enthusiastic and expressive	Can't remember names
Cheerful	Too happy for some
Curious	Egotistical
Good onstage	Naive, gets taken in
Wide-eyed and innocent	Has loud voice and laugh
Lives in the present	Controlled by circumstances
Sincere at heart	Gets angry easily
Always a child	Never grows up
As a Friend	*As a Friend*
Makes friends easily	Hates to be alone
Loves people	Wants to be center stage
Thrives on compliments	Looks for credit
Seems exciting	Dominates conversations
Doesn't hold grudges	Interrupts and doesn't listen
Apologizes quickly	Forgetful
Likes spontaneous activities	Repeats stories
At Work	*At Work*
Volunteers for jobs	Would rather talk
Thinks up new activities	Forgets obligations
Creative and colorful	Doesn't follow through
Has energy and enthusiasm	Undisciplined
Inspires others to join	Decides by feelings
Charms others to work	Easily distracted

THE POWERFUL CHOLERIC—
The Extrovert, The Doer, The Optimist

STRENGTHS	WEAKNESSES
Emotions	*Emotions*
Born leader	Bossy
Dynamic and active	Impatient
Must correct wrongs	Quick tempered
Decisive	Can't relax
Unemotional	Enjoys controversy
Not easily discouraged	Won't give up when losing
Independent	Comes on too strong
Exudes confidence	Inflexible
Can run anything	Unsympathetic
As a Friend	*As a Friend*
Has little need for friends	Tends to use people
Will work for group activity	Dominates others
Will lead and organize	Knows everything
Excels in emergencies	May be right, but unpopular
At Work	*At Work*
Goal oriented	Little tolerance for mistakes
Sees the whole picture	Doesn't analyze details
Organizes well	Bored by trivia
Seeks practical solutions	May make rash decisions
Moves quickly to action	May be rude or tactless
Delegates work	Manipulates people
Insists on production	Demanding of others
Stimulates activity	End justifies the means
Thrives on opposition	Work may become his god

THE PERFECT MELANCHOLY—
The Introvert, The Thinker, The Pessimist

STRENGTHS	WEAKNESSES
Emotions	*Emotions*
Deep and thoughtful	Remembers the negative
Analytical	Moody and depressed
Serious and purposeful	Has false sense of humility
Genius prone	Off in another world
Talented and creative	Low self-image
Artistic or musical	Self-centered
Philosophical and poetic	Too introspective
Sensitive to others	Guilt feelings
Conscientious	Persecution complex
Idealistic	Tends to be a hypochondriac
As a Friend	*As a Friend*
Makes friends cautiously	Lives through others
Content to stay in background	Insecure socially
Avoids causing attention	Withdrawn and remote
Faithful and devoted	Critical of others
Will listen to complaints	Holds back affection
Can solve others' problems	Dislikes those in opposition
Deep concern for other people	Suspicious of people
Compassionate	Unforgiving
Seeks ideal mate	Skeptical of compliments
At Work	*At Work*
Schedule oriented	Not people oriented
High standards	Depressed over imperfections
Detail conscious	Chooses difficult work
Persistent and thorough	Hesitant to start projects
Orderly and organized	Spends too much time planning
Neat and tidy	Prefers analysis to work
Economical	Hard to please
Sees the problem	Self-deprecating
Finds creative solutions	Standards often too high
Likes charts, graphs, lists	Deep need for approval

THE PEACEFUL PHLEGMATIC—
The Introvert, The Watcher, The Pessimist

STRENGTHS	WEAKNESSES
Emotions	*Emotions*
Low-key personality	Unenthusiastic
Easygoing and relaxed	Fearful and worried
Calm, cool, and collected	Indecisive
Patient, well balanced	Avoids responsibility
Consistent life	Quiet will of iron
Quiet but witty	Selfish
Sympathetic and kind	Too shy and reticent
Keeps emotions hidden	Too compromising
All-purpose person	Self-righteous
As a Friend	*As a Friend*
Easy to get along with	Dampens enthusiasm
Pleasant and enjoyable	Stays uninvolved
Inoffensive	Is not exciting
Good listener	Indifferent to plans
Dry sense of humor	Judges others
Has compassion and concern	Sarcastic and teasing
Has many friends	Resists change
At Work	*At Work*
Competent and steady	Not goal oriented
Peaceful and agreeable	Lacks self-motivation
Has administrative ability	Hard to get moving
Mediates problems	Resents being pushed
Avoids conflicts	Lazy and careless
Good under pressure	Discourages others
Finds the easy way	Would rather watch

**Taken from information in Florence Littauer's books, lectures, seminars with permission.

The popular sanguine, friendly, cheerful, a talker—can talk too much, elaborating and exaggerating. If operating in weaknesses, the powerful choleric who is confident and takes charge can be bossy, rude, and tactless. Did I say that I scored the highest in these two categories?

The perfect melancholy, detail conscious and genius prone, can carry those wonderful attributes to extreme and be a perfectionist who only remembers the negative. And the peaceful and easygoing phlegmatic can be *so* laid-back that there is no motivation whatsoever. Yes, these weaknesses can occasionally be seen in John.

Why did we each marry someone so strange?

On Time Every Time

You may wonder how soon those annoying weaknesses surface after you say, "I do." I am not sure if there is a standard amount of months, weeks, days, or hours, but I can tell you how it happened for us.

Within days of our wedding, John and I headed for Texas and pilot training for the United States Air Force. His schedule was very hectic. Mine was more laid back. The only day we really did anything together that involved a specific arrival time was Sunday morning church.

That first Sunday morning in Texas went something like this. . . . We got up and John announced that we would be leaving for the base chapel in fifty-five minutes. *Plenty of time*, I thought. I ate a bowl of cereal and then took a shower. The time kept ticking by as I dried my hair and put on a little makeup. The next thing I knew, John was rapping on the bathroom door and announcing, "We need to be in the car in 4 minutes and 37 seconds." I am not kidding you! I remember thinking to myself, *So that's why watches have a second hand.*

Moments later he returned with an update: "2 minutes and 30 seconds till we leave," he barked. At this point I didn't know whether to laugh or cry. Wow, this man was serious about time. Why hadn't I noticed that before? Honestly, I have no idea how many minutes or seconds it was before our car backed out of the driveway to head for church, but that was the day I learned that I had married a man who could not only *tell* time, but wanted to be *on* time. And there I was—a woman who wore a watch because it was pretty. Opposites attract.

We married each other's strengths, and now the weaknesses were getting in the way.

I have a very outgoing, optimistic personality. John is much more reserved. When we share the speaking platform, he has been known to say, "Kendra is here today making new friends. It's not that I don't like all of you, but, frankly, you wear me out."

John has a very peaceful phlegmatic personality with just a hint of melancholy perfectionism. It is a small hint, just a dab, and it surfaces mainly in the arena of timeliness. He is a quiet individual with occasional bursts of enthusiasm. I am an enthusiastic person with occasional bursts of calm. People truly do wear him out. They energize me. I am spontaneous. He is calculated.

The Influence of Gender

It is important to understand that the personalities are not linked to gender. In your home, it may be the husband who is the extrovert, a sanguine/choleric, and not the wife. Some of our best friends follow that pattern. Curt is outgoing and the life of the party. His wife, Pam, a phlegmatic/melancholy, is much more reserved.

I remember a conversation I had with Pam a few years ago. I was telling her about a wonderful idea I had . . . a wonderful, fantastic, spectacular idea . . . which is, by the way, the only kind the sanguine has, whether they are really good ideas or not. Pam listened intently, smiled occasionally, and nodded knowingly. When I finally paused to take a breath and looked at her for her approval, she simply said, "That's a very good idea."

My immediate reaction was disappointment. *Pam didn't like the idea*, I thought. What was wrong? Hadn't I explained it adequately?

Knowing me so well and loving me anyway, this dear friend continued in the next breath. "Kendra," Pam began, "you have to remember that I am a phlegmatic. I used the word *very*, and that is a lot of enthusiasm for me."

True, true. Pam was not one to waste time or energy on extra adjectives! Her husband and I cannot get enough adjectives in one sentence. Curt and I share similar personalities. Pam is more like John.

Lord, Change My Spouse!

I told you that I am an enthusiastic extrovert. If I carry that typical strength to extremes I am capable of being overbearing and generally obnoxious. Enough of that. Now I'm ready to get brutally honest about someone else's personality.

John's peaceful personality can sometimes morph into procrastination or such quiet resolve that he appears aloof and arrogant. When we married, it was easy for each of us to see the weakness in the other. And, unfortunately, we decided it was our duty to change the other person. This came to light one evening as we attended a party together.

I love parties, especially theme parties! John is generally not as enthusiastic about social gatherings, and on this particular evening, he attended the event rather reluctantly. I am guessing that part of his reluctance was the realization that because I was so excited about the event, the chances were great that the strengths of my personality— friendliness, enthusiasm, upbeat outlook, etc.—would be carried to extremes and he would be frustrated.

Unbeknownst to me, John had a plan to combat my potential "off the Richter scale" behavior. His plan was to get quieter. He just knew that as I witnessed him growing more and more quiet, I would get the message and quiet down myself.

I also had a plan. Because I knew that his quiet nature was capable of making people uncomfortable, I had decided that I would combat that by exuding more enthusiasm. Surely he would notice my increasingly upbeat attitude and make the appropriate adjustments.

Right now you might be asking yourself, "Were John and Kendra really that naive?" I guess the answer would be yes. And the answer to your next unspoken question, "Did this possibly work?" would be no.

John got quieter and I got noisier. I got noisier and John got quieter. It was a vicious, downward spiral. But, thankfully, it did culminate in a very honest conversation on the drive home. That conversation began the change in the way we operated. It was not a quiet and calm conversation, and it did not result in an immediate change, but it was the catalyst we needed. We were not loving or appreciating each other's personality strengths. We were not trying to improve in our areas of weakness. We were not doing our kids a favor.

Let's Talk

Our conversation that evening began with accusations and defensiveness.

"Why did you choose to be so quiet, so arrogant?"

"Why were you so talkative?"

"I was just trying to compensate for you!"

"Well that is exactly what I was doing!!"

Even though initially both of us adamantly defended our behavior, we were both willing to admit that it was an exaggeration of the norm. John was more quiet than usual and I was noisier. Although we claimed that these overstatements were legitimate, just acknowledging the truth that they *were* overstatements was step one.

The next step was to concede that our "over the top" reactions had not accomplished our goals. My increased talking had not encouraged John to be more talkative. His magnified quietness had not encouraged me to be quieter. In fact it was just the opposite. The truth was, our wonderful plans had failed miserably.

Then came the challenge to honestly evaluate the "why" of our actions. Were we embarrassed by each other? Maybe a little, but more important was the realization that we genuinely thought we could help each other. Taking correction is not always easy, but when given with love it can be a wonderful blessing. Maybe, just maybe we could help each other by sharing and teaching from our strengths. And then we could help our kids.

The Favors

As you and your spouse understand your personality differences and positively apply those differences in your parenting, you will be doing several favors for your kids.

Your child will:

1. Be capable of identifying his God-given personality with both its strengths and weaknesses.
2. Learn to develop those strengths and minimize the weaknesses.
3. Experience a positive model for marriage and healthy interper-

sonal relationships where personality strengths are appreciated and weaknesses are diminished.

Love Your Spouse

The attitude change that began that evening at the party and culminated in working together and learning from each other's strengths was very significant for John and me in loving each other. As you look at personality types and identify your personality, the challenge will be to focus on enhancing your personal strengths and tempering your weaknesses. Because you and your spouse will most likely have different personalities, the next task will be to learn how to love your spouse in spite of those differences. As you love your spouse, the one with that "opposite" personality, that strange person you married, you will be able to help your children identify and accept their personalities with their strengths and weaknesses.

In order to do this you will need to be a student of your child. Watch and listen as your son or daughter interacts with others. Is he outgoing or more reserved? Would she rather play alone or with others? Is he reticent to share his opinion? Is she leading the charge? By being attentive to your child's communication with others, verbal and nonverbal, you can usually determine his innate personality. When your child knows the God-given strengths he possesses because of his personality, he will gain confidence in who he is. God has chosen the personality for your child and He did not make a mistake.

Once your child's personality has been identified, you then have the ability to help your child appreciate his strengths and moderate his weaknesses. And your loving relationship with your spouse will give your child the opportunity to experience a positive model for marriage and healthy interpersonal relationships where personality strengths are appreciated and weaknesses are diminished.

Understand Your Kids

John and I were blessed with three sons with three distinct personalities. It was our responsibility to encourage each of them in their strengths. The sanguine entertainer, for example, was applauded for his quick wit and charming personality. The easygoing phlegmatic son was admired for his ability to adapt to any and every situation. The born leader, the choleric, was appreciated for his goal-oriented actions. They each learned to value the strengths of their own personalities and those of others.

While encouraging their personality strengths, we were also able to help them identify and temper their weaknesses. When we noticed that our sanguine entertainer was using his wit in a hurtful way, we gently pointed that out to him and he learned not to carry his quick wit into the realm of hurtful sarcasm. Sometimes we had to encourage our easygoing son to stretch and reach out to others rather than to rest. His natural tendency was not to get involved even when he knew that could be a better choice. With our encouragement he learned that there were times, be it ever so painful, for direct action. As parents, we made sure our born leader realized that demanding too much of others did not achieve the goals he had established. He learned that his way was not always the only way.

As you love your spouse with his or her opposite personality, your children will be affirmed in their God-given temperaments, which may be like yours or your spouse's. They will see an example of someone who is at work tempering his or her weaknesses. And your relationship will illustrate a positive model for marriage.

A positive model for marriage and other interpersonal relationships does not suggest the lack of conflict. There will be times in everyone's life when personality differences will cause disagreements. Interestingly enough, the clash occurs not only between people who have been graced with opposite personalities, but also with those whose personalities are more similar. It is almost as though the annoying traits each of us possess are magnified when we see them in someone else. That is the time to remember that in order to have any positive relationships in life, you must allow the other person at least three glaring faults. In marriage you might want to allow a few more.

Apply the Knowledge

When our kids were still in elementary school, we began to teach them about the personality types. Before long they were able to identify strengths and weaknesses in their own lives and in the lives of others. What a great tool for them at an early age.

One day our son Aaron told me that his math teacher was "very melancholy."

"How do you know?" I asked.

"She announced that the decimal point had to be *right on the line*, not above it or below it," he answered.

"So," I said, "what are you going to do?"

"Put it on the line, of course!" was the reply. And I'm sure that saved him several red marks on his math papers . . . all because he understood the personality types, his own and others.

Because John and I are so different, and because we were learning to appreciate the strengths of each other, we could honestly communicate appreciation for our personalities and the different personalities of each of our children.

What Not to Do

My father was forty-five years old when I was born, and he referred to me on many occasions as his "built-in grandchild." That title definitely had some positives and some negatives. My father was very lenient with me when I was growing up. I used to consider that as something totally in the plus column, but looking back, I would have benefited greatly from a little more "hands on" parenting from him—in every sense of the phrase. Being the baby of the family is a position I wouldn't want to change, but coupled with my personality, I know there were times when I completely exhausted my dad.

Because of that fact, I heard a lot of statements like "Quit running." "Don't talk so loudly." "Settle down." "Be quiet." Those far outweighed statements like "I love you." "That was a very creative solution!" "Come over here and sit by me." My dad was just too tired and also slightly disinterested.

Add to that the fact that he and I had very similar personalities. He was also outgoing and optimistic. Because of the almost constant conflict between my mother and my father, I am guessing that she found my carbon copy personality annoying too. So I had one parent who was too tired to appreciate my enthusiasm and one parent who didn't want me to remind her of the other. Can you see how this situation is far from achieving our three favors? There was very little acceptance of the personality differences.

If my personality paralleled my father's, what did my mother's look like? She was a borderline perfectionist, a melancholy, with the perfect routine and system for everything. To her credit, she did not demand that I operate under the same high standards that she did, but she did have a "rule" for everything. And here I am—the offspring of these two people, who constantly wondered why they had married each other.

Was I taught that my personality was one to be valued? No, I was not. In fact for many years I wished I were the quiet wallflower that they both seemed to prefer. I would prepare to go to a party and decide that this would be the evening when I would be quiet and stand back in the recesses of the action. And that resolution would hold until I arrived and took my coat off. Then my natural tendencies took over—sometimes to the extreme.

I did not feel good about how God had created me with my specific personality. I was under the impression that I had plenty of weaknesses but no strengths. My parents failed to help me:

1. Identify my God-given personality, realizing the strengths and weaknesses,
2. Learn to develop those strengths and moderate the weaknesses, or
3. Experience a positive model for marriage and healthy interpersonal relationships where personality strengths are appreciated and weaknesses are diminished.

Rather than appreciate the personality strengths of others, I coveted them.

Now What?

The good news is that regardless of your childhood experiences you can learn to accept your personality and to love that strange spouse of yours with the opposite personality. Let's walk through the process.

God's Word is clear. You are to "love the Lord your God with all your heart and with all your soul and with all your mind" (Matt. 22:37). And "love your neighbor as yourself" (Matt. 22:39). Loving yourself is not an arrogant or self-centered love. We are to love ourselves as a creation of God. We are to look for His love within us and share that with others. God loves us and that gives us the ability to love Him and to love our neighbor and ourselves. I learned that in order to do that I needed to:

- Understand and accept my outgoing sanguine personality as a gift from God, appreciating my strengths and accepting the challenge to temper my weaknesses.
- Understand and accept John's personality as a gift from God, encouraging him in his strengths and as he worked to diminish his weaknesses.

The ability to do this came with maturity and with living out the knowledge of Christ's love. The more love and acceptance I felt from John, the more I understood God's love, which far exceeded even that of my loving husband. As John and I learned to encourage each other in our strengths, I was able to accept the personality God had given me. Ask yourself—are you doing what you can do to lovingly support your spouse? Are you learning to appreciate the strengths of his or her personality? Are you overlooking *at least* three glaring faults? Those sorts of things can go a long way in helping your spouse understand and accept his or her personality.

Your Turn

By now you have probably determined the type of personality that God gave to you and also the one He gave to your spouse. Maybe you have also identified the personalities of your kids. Now is the time to take note of the things you like about your own personality. Then do the same with the personality of that strange person you married and with your kids. Share with each of them the strengths of their personalities that you see illustrated in their lives. Help them to enhance their natural strengths and to appreciate the positive attributes they see in other people. They may even choose to develop some strengths that do not come as naturally to them.

Our two extroverted sons have no problem taking charge in a situation when necessary. Our more introverted son has the same ability—but not by nature. He learned that skill by seeing that strength in his sanguine/choleric mother and brothers and learning to appreciate it. And all of us have profited from developing the ability to think before we speak. Guess who we learned that one from? You're right! John, the phlegmatic/melancholy.

God has instructed you to love Him and to love your neighbor. There is no closer neighbor than those in your own household. It is reassuring to know that God will never ask you to do something that He will not empower you to do. He will help you do your kids a favor and love your spouse.

A Good Word from John, the Resident Dad

The first complete chapter of the Bible that I memorized was Psalm 139. I was intrigued by the feeling of God's closeness and by His attention to detail in the verses.

> O Lord, you have searched me and you know me. You know when I sit and when I rise; you perceive my thoughts from afar. You discern my going out and my lying down; you are familiar with all my ways. Before a word is on my tongue you know it completely, O Lord. You hem me in—behind and before; you have laid your hand upon me. (Psalm 139:1–5)

It continues in verses 13 and 14.

> For you created my inmost being; you knit me together in my mother's womb. I praise you because I am fearfully and wonderfully made.

These verses from the book of Psalms are very appropriate to finish our chapter on personalities. Actually, they apply to each and every chapter of *Do Your Kids a Favor.* God knit us together. We are fearfully and wonderfully made. This includes the personality He has woven into our being.

Loving Kendra with her outgoing personality was not always easy for me. In the first few years of our marriage, I decided that it was one of her shortcomings. I was wrong. Instead it turned out to be a wonderful asset. She communicates very effectively and has blessed many thousands through her writing and speaking. And even more important to me, her effervescent ways filled our home with laughter and fun. When I understood that God made each of us and our personalities, it helped me understand and love Kendra the way God made her.

Enjoying, using, and honing the strengths while diminishing the weaknesses of our personalities was a favor we chose to do for our kids. It was a part of loving each other. Our sons learned as we learned. They watched our personality clashes and the resolution of those disagreements. They enjoyed their mom's extroverted ways. They learned to enjoy other people. They laughed when she got a little wound up and helped her bring that energy and enthusiasm under control again.

They also took note of my quieter, introverted manner. It was a bit upsetting for them when I would withdraw and get very quiet. Along with their mom, they helped me see the error of my ways. If I remember correctly, my behavior was fondly referred to as pouting. Hmmm . . .

It is easy to see how parents who love each other enough to learn about both of their personalities do their kids a favor. It is important to develop the strengths of each personality while diminishing the weaknesses.

Our kids had a head start when they left our home, having identified their personalities and having learned to appreciate the personalities of others. Your kids can have a head start too! Remember, God knit you together in your mother's womb. He did the same for your spouse. God does not make mistakes. Do your kids a favor. Love your spouse.

What's Next?

Do you remember packing for your honeymoon? For me it was a big deal. I wanted to look lovely every minute of every day, so I packed my bags with great care. What I did not know was that I was also bringing some baggage into our marriage that I had unknowingly packed and some that had been packed for me . . . baggage that could make it difficult to love my husband. I was carrying a lot more into our relationship than I ever imagined. I was surprised to discover the answer to the question, "What did you pack besides lingerie?" Maybe you will be too.

Time for Some Honest Evaluation

1. When you read the descriptions of the personalities, how did you primarily classify yourself? Sanguine? Choleric? Melancholy? Or Phlegmatic? What about your spouse?

2. What is one of your personality strengths? Now name a personality strength of your spouse—one you especially appreciate.

3. What is one of your weaknesses? What are you doing to temper that weakness? Don't answer for your spouse, just for yourself.

4. What is the primary personality of each of your children?

5. Are any of your kids "just like you"? Does that enhance your relationship, or is it a detriment? Is one of your kids a carbon copy of your spouse? Does that enhance your relationship, or is it a detriment?

6. Think of one way you can communicate to your children the value of their strengths. How can you help your children appreciate the personality strengths of an opposite personality?

7. Because every personality type has weaknesses too, it will be your responsibility to help your child diminish his weaknesses. Think of one weakness in your child that could use some work. Now lovingly and gently help your child understand that this could be an area of improvement. As you see that improvement, be sure to applaud it heartily!

CHAPTER FOUR

Unpacking the Baggage: What Did I Pack Besides Lingerie?

Several years ago I flew into Lehigh Valley International Airport in Bethlehem, Pennsylvania for a speaking engagement. With only carry-on luggage, I breezed down to the lower level of the airport to get my rental car. After filling out the paperwork, I asked the attendant if she could provide me with a map for my journey. When I told her my destination, she replied with a question. "Oh," she said, smiling, "are you going there to shop the outlets?"

"I am now," I replied.

And shop I did. I didn't just settle for outlet prices, I went to the clearance racks in the outlet stores. It was February, but I did a great majority of my Christmas shopping in the next two days. Finally it was time to return home. I loaded all my purchases into my rental car and headed for the airport.

Would you believe me if I told you that I did not think about the fact that my backseat was loaded with shopping bags . . . until I parked in the rental car lot? Then it dawned on me—I should have purchased a suitcase! How in the world would I get all these things home?

My carry-on luggage became drag-on luggage. I squished and squeezed and squashed and crushed all my belongings, new and old, and ultimately put everything inside of the rolling bag. That was the day

I discovered that a nightie can fit into a toothbrush holder if you try hard enough.

I made it home that evening and all was intact, except maybe the back of the kindly gentleman who asked if I'd like assistance putting my bag in the overhead compartment. My luggage was full! My baggage was heavy and I was very thankful that I didn't have to drag it around for more than one flight.

Unfortunately some folks have baggage that is even heavier and more unwieldy than my drag-on luggage. I'm talking about emotional baggage, not airline luggage. They may have packed the contents themselves or had their bags packed for them. But whether bags were packed for us or by us, and whether they are heavy or light, God can help unpack any baggage we might carry.

The Favors

As a spouse and parent, it is important that you engage in the unpacking process. When you invest the time and energy in this process, you will be doing three important favors for your child.

Your child will:

1. Learn to honestly identify baggage.
2. Avoid the transferring of some of your cumbersome baggage into his life.
3. Experience a positive model for marriage and healthy interpersonal relationships and for the unpacking process.

Why Bother?

You might imagine that the purpose of eliminating the baggage is to make the journey of life more pleasant. That is a great residual benefit, but more important, you unpack baggage so that you are better equipped to do your kids a favor and love your spouse. Personally I have become a more loving spouse as my bags have gotten lighter.

Furthermore, because I have engaged in the sometimes painful, usually productive process of unpacking baggage, my children have witnessed me honestly identifying my personal baggage. They saw a model of husband and wife working together to lovingly eliminate baggage before it was transferred to the next generation . . . a positive model for marriage and healthy interpersonal relationships. It is important to note that baggage that remains with you usually finds its way, in some form or other, into your children's bags, making it more difficult to do your kids a favor. So unpack those bags.

My Personal Baggage

In my early years as a mom, I read that we are all the product of imperfect parents. I hated to think about that in my role as a mother, but when I put on my "childhood hat," I knew that it was true.

I grew up in a small town in the middle of America, the youngest of three children. Our standards for honesty, justice, morality, and language were high. Church did not play a significant part in our family life. It was not a Christian home.

My father was a dentist and a pillar of the community (whatever that is). My mom was a homemaker. Like many married couples, they were as different as night and day. Mom was regimented and melancholy. Dad was a fun-loving sanguine. In his dental practice his philosophy was, "If you have a problem I'll be glad to help you. Later on we'll determine how you will pay for the work." Dad was a generous and kind man . . . and he was an alcoholic.

I was raised in the home of an alcoholic. That made me the product of a dysfunctional home. For many years I didn't realize what a large club I was a part of! I never heard the term *dysfunctional* when I was growing up. In fact, I really didn't think that my home was much different from anyone else's. I once heard someone describe a dysfunctional home as a home with a dead elephant in the middle of the living room floor. This elephant has been there forever, and the family simply ignores it and walks around it rather than attempting to clean it up. That is actually a pretty accurate description—both the craziness of it and the acceptance of that craziness as normal. Yes, I had a dead elephant in my life, and the space that it consumed gave me negative baggage even though I thought I was able to ignore the problem.

So how did having an alcoholic father affect me? To this day, I am still discovering the answers to that question. Probably the most negative and most significant was the feeling that no adult in our household cared much about me. That was my perception, not necessarily reality. My parents were involved in their own worlds, their own struggles, their own war. Too many times I was left outside of their lives and felt unloved, unnecessary, and invisible. That phenomenon helped to create one selfish young lady. Unconsciously I believed that if I did not look out for myself, no one else would. Selfishness is very heavy baggage to drag through your life. And what is worse, it tends to become part of your children's baggage, part of their inheritance. I was determined not to pass on the influence of alcoholism to my children. I resolved not to drink, not to pack that in their luggage. However, I had inadvertently packed another harmful behavior. It was selfishness.

Selfishness was not the only unconstructive thing I packed in my luggage of life. From my point of view as a child, my father's alcoholism controlled our lives and dictated everything I did, from the friends I had over to the activities I engaged in. Because of that, his alcoholism brought a great deal of anger. In our family, openly displaying anger or aggression was not allowed—no stomping or hitting or verbal explosions. Hence I developed a more "socially acceptable" means of expressing my anger. I honed the skill of sarcasm. (And I use the word *skill* sarcastically.)

I believe that anger expressed in sarcasm is just as harmful as, per-haps even more than, anger expressed physically. You cannot dodge a sarcastic remark, and the pain and scar can be devastating. I realized, not soon enough, that being witty was one thing and being hurtful with sarcastic words was another. I wanted my children to be creative and clever, but not mean and malicious with their words.

Packed for Me and by Me

Alcoholism was heavy baggage put into my luggage of life by some-one else. Unfortunately I added additional destructive behavior and my bags got heavier. As a parent, I loved my children and was acutely aware of the possibility of transferring the weight to them. I had to unload some of my negative baggage before it was shifted to my children. I real-ized that even if I chose never to drink a drop of alcohol, I could still weigh down my kids with overflow from my own negative reactions to alcoholism. Ultimately, it didn't really matter who had packed the bag-gage; it was the unpacking that was important.

More Heavy Baggage

Alcoholism is my example of heavy baggage packed for me. That example may not apply to you, but other possibilities might. Any type of abuse or abandonment—physical, mental, or emotional—creates baggage. Sexual abuse or drug abuse in a home can also lead to heavy baggage for the abuser and the innocent child. Your parents' divorce could fall into the category of heavy baggage packed for you. When any of these things happen, the chances are great that the load will become even heavier when you add negative things as you react to the negative things packed for you.

We contribute to the weight of our own bags when we make poor decisions about alcohol and drug use. Choices about sexual involvement can result in heavy baggage, as can divorce or the previous divorce of your spouse. Many times, these choices, while packed personally by you, are the reaction to the baggage packed for you.

But always remember—the question of *who* did the packing is not as important as taking the challenge to begin the unpacking process. It is your responsibility as a parent. Your family is counting on you. It is a part of loving your spouse. He or she can aid the process of unpacking.

How to Unpack

Maybe you agree that negative baggage is harmful, but you are wondering how you can start the process of unpacking. Simple steps will begin the elimination process. Notice I said "simple" steps, not easy ones.

1. Admit that baggage exists.
2. Realize that the baggage has negatively influenced your behavior and your relationship with your spouse and your kids.
3. Forgive the person who packed the baggage.
4. Keep moving forward in the process.

Let's look at each of these steps as I share my personal walk through the process.

Admit That Baggage Exists

Believe it or not, it never occurred to me that my father was an alcoholic until one evening early in our marriage. Sure, I knew that he drank, but I thought an alcoholic was someone who couldn't hold down a job. An alcoholic couldn't possibly be a "pillar of the community." Furthermore, I was certain that alcoholics didn't have families with respectable kids. And undoubtedly most alcoholics lived in big cities and drank cheap stuff hidden in a paper bag.

That is precisely what I *used* to think. But I was not correct in my thinking. Alcoholics come from every walk of life. They are fathers and mothers and brothers and sisters and sons and daughters. Alcoholism is so widespread that many of you reading this book have been directly touched by it.

Now, back to the beginning of the unpacking process. John and I were newlyweds and he was attending pilot training for the United States Air Force. We had met a couple at chapel one Sunday and invited them to dinner. In the course of the conversation, the gentleman said that his mother was coming for a visit the next week, and that she was an alcoholic.

After they left and John and I were doing dishes, I broached the subject. "Isn't that *awful* that his mother is an alcoholic?" I said with some degree of emotion.

John looked quite surprised and innocently replied, "Kendra, your dad is an alcoholic."

That was all it took. My emotions skyrocketed. I couldn't believe that John was saying such a cruel thing. "That's not true!" I blurted out. "Don't ever say that again!"

He dropped the subject, but I couldn't forget his words. Was my dad an alcoholic? I wasn't even sure I knew what that word meant. Even though John and I did not discuss it any further for days and days, it was continually on my mind. I knew I needed information and answers, so I went into my fact-finding mode. I wanted to find out the specifics about alcoholism.

John's words as a loving spouse became the stimulus I needed to begin the process of truthful evaluation. I had only recently become a Christian and I knew very little about the Word of God. But years later, I have come to treasure the words of John 8:32, "You will know the truth, and the truth will set you free." That is what was happening in my life. As I searched and thought and prayed and contemplated, I discovered, quite reluctantly, the truth of what my husband had said. Ultimately I was able to admit that I had the baggage of having an alcoholic father. That truth, so gently and lovingly suggested by John, was the first step in the unpacking process, the process that would set me free and free my children from that particular weighty baggage.

"You are my lamp, O Lord; the Lord turns my darkness into light."

(2 SAMUEL 22:29

Realize That the Baggage Has Negatively Influenced Behavior and Relationships

John likes to say, "Kendra can detect a thimbleful of near-beer a block away." And he is pretty close to accurate. Smelling any alcohol on my father was an instant trigger. My attitude transformed almost immediately. I became angry and sarcastic and mean-spirited toward my father. I showed no compassion or caring . . . no kindness to him in any form. I used to say that Dad was like Jekyll and Hyde. When he was sober he was a joy to be around. When he was drunk he was just the opposite. After I started dealing in the truth, I realized that I, too, was like Jekyll and Hyde—kind and loving when he was sober, and the complete opposite when he had been drinking. Furthermore, it was hard to admit, but the negative baggage I had packed in response to his alcoholism was rearing its ugly head even when he was nowhere around. Take a look at 2 Corinthians 2:5–8 with me.

If anyone has caused grief, he has not so much grieved me as he has grieved all of you, to some extent—not to put it too severely. The punishment inflicted on him by the majority is sufficient for him. Now instead, you ought to forgive and comfort him, so that he will not be overwhelmed by excessive sorrow. I urge you, therefore, to reaffirm your love for him.

I could not continue to punish my father for his alcoholism. I needed to unpack selfishness and sarcasm from my baggage. I had to realize that it was negatively influencing my behavior and my relationship with John and potentially with my kids.

Forgive the Person Who Packed the "Baggage"

Look at verses 10–11 in 2 Corinthians 2.

If you forgive anyone, I also forgive him. And what I have forgiven—if there was anything to forgive—I have forgiven in the sight of Christ for your sake, in order that Satan might not outwit us. For we are not unaware of his schemes.

God was calling me to forgive. To me the most amazing thing is the phrase at the end of verse 10—three little words—"for your sake." God encourages us to forgive for our *own* sake, for the well-being of us as individuals, as husbands and wives, and ultimately as parents. Verse 11 reminds us that Satan has schemes and that his desire is for us to fall victim to those. Don't be outwitted. Extend forgiveness. I had to deal with the fact that baggage packed for me and by me was negatively influencing my behavior and my interactions. Then I needed to choose to forgive the ones who packed it for me.

Keep Moving Forward in the Process

When I was first able and willing to admit that I was raised in the home of an alcoholic, it didn't occur to me that I would want, need, or be willing someday to forgive my father for being an alcoholic. That transition happened in the most supernatural way.

Back Home Again

John's schedule in pilot training was rigorous and he was gone a great deal. After much prayer, he and I made the decision that I would return to my parents' home for the last portion of his training and that I would enroll for another semester toward my college degree. Mom and Dad agreed to have their empty nest filled once again, and so I headed for their home. My mission was twofold: to finish one more semester at the university and to share the gospel with my father. After all, I reasoned, he needed Jesus more than anyone did! In truth, an alcoholic is in as dire need of Jesus as is every other human being. (See appendix for some solid theology . . . what Jesus has done for our salvation.)

I soon learned that my semester at school was the easy part of my mission. To the best of my memory, my father had always resisted the gospel message. I remember hearing him say, "All the church people want is my money."

If I was to effectively share my love of Jesus with my dad, I knew I had to have a plan. I remembered hearing, "You may be the only Bible someone ever reads," and I realized that my actions and responses to Dad were going to be very important. That and prayer! Every evening I took time to visit with my father, whether he had been drinking or not. My job was to be Christ's representative to Dad, and I took the difficult assignment seriously. I bit my tongue when I wanted to react with a sarcastic comment. I chose instead to respond in a calm and considerate way. After our visit each evening I prayed that God would change my father.

As a new believer, I was learning simple truths about God and the Christian walk. One thing that I was sure of was that God loved me and that He wanted everyone to love Him too. Night after night I prayed for Dad, asking God to change him. Then one night I stopped speaking and actually tried to listen. It wasn't an audible voice that I heard, but as certainly as I was aware of my location, I was aware of who was giving me the thoughts I was having.

"Kendra, how about if you let Me change you?"

What? I thought. *I'm not the alcoholic, Dad is. God, You need to change him!*

"Let's not worry about your dad right now. Let Me change you."

Now I already told you that I was definitely a beginner when it came to having a relationship with the Lord. There was, however, one thing I was certain of, and that was that God was smarter than I was.

"OK, Lord, please change me." That became my new prayer. And slowly but surely, God answered that prayer. One night as I prepared to go to sleep after an evening visit with my dad, I found myself thanking God for the change He had made in my father's life. *Look across the hall to your dad's bedroom,* the thought came. *Do you see a change?*

No, there was no evidence of change . . . no noticeable difference in my dad's behavior. Yet something was different. I was different. I did not have the feelings of hostility that I typically had when he had been drinking, as he had been on that particular evening. I did not have to try so hard to curb my tongue when we had our time together. Instead the desire to be sarcastic and my feelings of anger, disappointment, and grief had been miraculously replaced by God's love. God had answered my prayer. He had changed me. The change had been slow and gradual, but it had occurred!

I don't know whether my dad ever came to know Jesus, but John had a chance to share his faith with Dad, and he had the opportunity.

In Everything Give Thanks

Years later, after my dad's death, I was addressing a group of women at a pastors' wives retreat. As I prayed to close a session where I had shared the story of my father, I heard myself say, "I'm thankful that my dad was my dad." What? Where did those words come from? More important, where did that genuine attitude come from? The answer was from God. He had given me forgiveness. It had been a process.

What about the forgiveness I needed to extend to myself for the ugly things *I* had packed in my bags? That has been more difficult, but there has been progress. I am certain that "he who began a good work in [me] will carry it on to completion" (Phil. 1:6).

Why did I bother to take the time to admit that I had negative baggage in my life and that it had influenced my behavior? Why should you bother to do the same? It takes a great deal of energy to recognize your baggage and to persevere in the process of unpacking. A person has to wonder if all that work is really worthwhile.

If questions like that are on your mind, consider one additional question: If you could lighten the load in life for your son or daughter, would you be willing? Do you love your child enough? I knew you did!

Your children are the primary *why* in answer to all those questions. They are *why* you face the baggage in your life. They are *why* you deal with the negative influence that baggage has had on you and your decisions. They are *why* you forgive. The reason you bother is your kids. They are counting on you. And you and your spouse will benefit too.

Many years ago I decided that I needed to walk several times a week in order to get an adequate amount of exercise. One day when my oldest son was home from college, he accompanied me on my morning hike. He rode a bicycle and I walked. Besides keeping me company on my trek, he decided his role was to motivate me to greater achievement, which he determined was faster speed.

"Mom," he said at one point, "you really *could* go faster."

Realizing the truth in his words I simply replied, "Yes, I *could*, but speed is not my goal. I'm into longevity. I want to still be walking several times a week in ten years. If I go too fast, I'll get too tired and probably quit."

Help!

Unpacking the baggage is a process. Speed is not the goal. The goal is forward progress. You may find that you need help in the process of unpacking. Your spouse can be an amazing resource to help you to identify and unpack baggage. A Christian counselor or psychologist is a possible help as well. Your pastor may also be able to help. And never downplay prayer and the power of the Word of God. Memorizing Scripture hides it in your heart. Many of the forward steps in my own process were aided by Christian books in which the Word of God was the backbone of the teaching. Perhaps you are blessed with a trusted friend who loves you and wants you to succeed. If that is the case, this friend might also be able to encourage you and assist you in the unpacking process.

You can persevere and be a victor. You do not have to be a victim. Sure, you have had unpleasant circumstances in your life, but as you admit that truth, and acknowledge that the baggage has negatively influenced your behavior, you can find the strength to forgive. That begins the process toward victory. We are not victims, we are victors, taking seriously the responsibility and privilege of parenting future victors . . . great kids who love God, obey God, and glorify Him with their lives.

A Good Word from John, the Resident Dad

My baggage was not heavy. I grew up the second of four children. When I was young my dad was a schoolteacher, and until I was in junior high, my mom was a stay-at-home mom. I was loved, encouraged, corrected, and churched. When I was seven years old my dad made the decision to quit teaching school and become a full-time farmer. He farmed two hundred acres and had a hog operation. This involved many labor-intensive hours. I learned how to work at a very early age.

My mom and dad had an agreement. Dad would take care of the outside duties and Mom was in charge of everything inside. Dad's work, the "outside work," took precedence because it was providing for our livelihood. If Dad needed Mom to go to the machinery dealer for parts, she went without any discussion. There seemed to be no negotiating, nor were there many "pleases" and "thank-yous" in the mix. When we came inside to Mom's domain for dinner, we sat at the table and she waited on us, giving us what we requested. Again not many "pleases" or "thank-yous" filled the air.

Kendra brought this to my attention shortly after we were married. If I remember correctly the scenario went something like this. We were sitting at the kitchen table and I needed ketchup for my sandwich so I simply said, "Ketchup!"

After I repeated my demand, assuming she had not heard me, she reminded me that I had two good legs and could get my own ketchup. Undoubtedly it was the lack of courtesy that registered with her. She had identified some of the light baggage I was carrying. After I stood and got the ketchup we had a discussion about the necessity of basic consideration for others.

The process of unpacking light baggage is the same as for heavy baggage, and your spouse can help.

I admitted that this baggage existed and realized that it had, indeed, negatively influenced my behavior. Kendra did not find it difficult to forgive in this instance, and I truly thought that the case was closed and the process was completed.

I *thought* that was true until years later. After pilot training and my career flying for the USAF for several years, Kendra and I moved to a farm near where I grew up. At that time, I was hired to teach school and I also became a part-time farmer. Little did I know that farming would be the impetus that pushed me back into toting that inconsiderate behavior in my baggage. One day in the middle of planting season I went into the house for lunch. Our sons had gathered around the table, and as we started the meal one of them suddenly gave a one-word order to his mother for something he felt he needed. Kendra was taken aback by his rudeness and immediately corrected him.

"It's OK, Mom," the explanation began. "I was just being a farmer."

Now where had he learned that? Unfortunately the answer was from watching me, his dad. I had allowed that negative baggage to slip back into my life. I guess Kendra and I were so busy we had not noticed. The incident embarrassed me. I realized that not only was I treating Kendra disrespectfully, but our children were watching. It was light, but I knew I didn't want to pack that same baggage for them. I did not want them to treat their wives the way I was, once again, treating Kendra. I was not loving her as I should and not doing our kids a favor. Beware, baggage can sometimes mysteriously return.

> "The mocker seeks wisdom and finds none, but knowledge comes easily to the discerning."
>
> (PROVERBS 14:6)

Identifying and unpacking light baggage may not seem to be as difficult as dealing with the heavy stuff. *Sometimes* it is even more difficult because of our ability to dismiss and ignore it. Baggage, light or heavy, affects your marriage relationship, which in turn affects your children.

Take a look. Maybe you thought your bags were empty. Check the side pockets for lighter things. Your spouse could probably help you identify an item or two that might be hiding. Then work together on unpacking.

Be a discerning parent, obtaining godly knowledge in order to raise great kids—kids who love God, obey God, and glorify Him with their lives.

Impossible?

Because of his professional position, a gentleman we know was called to be in the courtroom at the sentencing of a young man who had been convicted of molesting two boys. It was a sad day for everyone involved—the repentant criminal and his family, his friends and those of the young boys, the family of those boys, and most of all the children themselves. Tears fell down our friend's cheeks as he described the courtroom situation. Sadness and remorse hung profoundly in the air as various people shared shame, guilt, regret, anger, and sorrow.

One person's words particularly disturbed our friend. This woman declared, "These young boys' lives have been ruined and there is no hope for their future."

My friend, a God-focused believer, said he wanted to stop the proceedings and declare, "What has been done was indeed monstrous and atrocious, but God's grace is greater than anything! His grace is greater than the pain these boys and their families have suffered, and He is capable and willing to do the impossible and heal the hurts of the past for both the victims and the guilty party." How true! How very, very true.

No one's baggage is ever so heavy that God is not capable of making the load lighter. Mine is not and neither is yours. Your child's will not be either. Our God is ready, willing, and able to take you from where you are right now (or where you have been) to where you need to be to serve and glorify Him. And the unpacking of that baggage, packed by you or for you, will strengthen your marriage and strengthen your parenting.

Time for Some Honest Reflection

Reflecting on the baggage in your life is a little like talking about garbage . . . it's stinky, it's rotten, and it's far from "table talk." But honestly identifying it is important in order to love your spouse and do your kids a favor. So . . .

1. As you read this chapter, could you relate to any of the examples of baggage, heavy or light, that were mentioned? Identify one thing that was packed for you as a child that you would like to unpack.

2. Undoubtedly you packed some things yourself, baggage that is weighing you down. What is one thing you personally packed that you need to begin eliminating?

3. Who do you need to forgive, regardless of whether they deserve or desire your forgiveness?

4. Is the baggage too heavy to unpack on your own? Seek a Christian counselor or pastor.

CHAPTER FIVE

Family Traditions:
You Call THAT Normal?

nor·mal [**nawr**-m*uh*l]
—adjective

1. conforming to the standard or the common type; usual; not abnormal; regular; natural.
2. serving to establish a standard.

The above definition comes directly from Dictionary.com. For most people it is probably slightly incomplete. Perhaps an illustration would be helpful. You know, like the one by the definition of armadillo in Webster's Dictionary of the English Language.

In case you have never seen one of these odd little animals, the dictionary is helpful enough to give a picture. So what picture would be featured by the definition of normal? Why, of course, a picture of you and your family. It doesn't matter how bizarre your family may be; in your eyes they are probably nor-

armadillo [ahr-*muh*-dil-oh]
n. any of a number of related toothless, burrowing mammals of Texas and Central and South America, having an armor-like covering of bony plates.

mal. As a married person, you brought your normal into the relationship and your spouse brought his or hers. There is no problem with that except for the fact that each normal is different.

I used to joke that our sons thought that our household was normal until they got married. Then their wives told them, "Your parents are not normal." Did this actually happen? I'm not sure, and I probably don't really want to know.

The point is this—in order to do your kids a favor and love your spouse, it is important for you to realize that the "normals" each of you brings into your marriage will have to be adjusted to create your new normal. One family's habits or traditions are not right and another family's wrong. They are merely different. Each spouse has to be willing to dialogue about the differences in a nondefensive, nonjudgmental way to achieve the goal of a loving compromise. That compromise will create the normal for your kids.

The Favors

It is important to adapt to each other's normal as Mom and Dad and to adjust to create a new normal for your own family. In doing that you will be loving your spouse and doing your child more than one favor.

Your child will:

1. Realize that traditions can be different and they are not necessarily wrong or right.
2. Learn the skill and importance of reaching a new normal.
3. Experience a positive model for marriage and healthy interpersonal relationships where family traditions are evaluated and compromises are made.

The question is: Are you willing to take the time, effort, and energy to create that new normal? Too many times couples have chosen, consciously or unconsciously, to allow the differences to remain. This means that there will be continued friction between husband and wife, mom and dad. In cases like that, each spouse is *sure* that his or her normal really *is* normal, and both are determined to hold out until they win. Well, while waiting for a win, they are losing big time. The kids are paying a price. Do your kids a favor and love your spouse by working together to establish the normal for your family.

How does that happen? How can a new normal be created?

The Big Inning

John and I and our three sons had taken our seats at Wrigley Field in Chicago. It was the first major league baseball game the kids had been to, but it would not be the last. I can't remember who the Cubs were playing, but honestly it does not matter when you have the opportunity to enjoy a great day at a great ballpark.

By the fifth inning, the boys were getting a little restless. When the hot-dog vendor came by, I signaled him and got a treat for each of the kids. I also got them something to drink. Little did I know, John was beside himself as the dogs and the cups of cold drinks were passed to where we were seated. In my world, my behavior—the purchasing of a hot dog and a soda pop at a sporting event—was quite normal. In John's world, it was just the opposite.

When we returned to the car after the game, he almost exploded. What in the world was I doing spending money on food at a ballpark? Those hot dogs that cost $2.50 each were worth about ten cents. That's what it would cost to make them at home. The pop was absolutely unnecessary! The game was only three hours and ten minutes long. No one was going to starve or die of thirst in that time.

To say that his reaction to my "shopping spree" shocked me would have been an understatement. What I had done was perfectly normal! That's what my family did. We enjoyed the food that was served by the vendors. We had a cold drink. Why, we even purchased a pennant to remember the day. What was the big deal?

The big deal was that John's normal prohibited the purchase of anything except a ticket. That was enough. All the rest was unnecessary. It was like throwing money away. I never knew that. No one had told me.

So what did we do after the smoke (coming out of John's ears) settled? We started to discuss what had actually caused the ruckus. After some searching, we determined that the conflict existed totally because of our different "normals" colliding.

A New Normal

When you and your spouse encounter a clash like we did on that day . . . when the behavior of your spouse doesn't seem to make sense or isn't normal, that is the time to get to the root of the conflict. The chances are great you are experiencing a discrepancy in your "normals." If that is the case, then consider these steps for reconciliation.

Step 1: Identify the source of the problem as the difference in your family traditions, your "normals."

Step 2: Recognize that standing firm, holding your ground, being right, is probably not the best thing for your relationship with your spouse or the best thing for your kids.

Step 3: Brainstorm with your spouse about possible solutions for a compromise. Create a new normal for your family.

John and I realized that he was not "wrong," and neither was I. We had different traditions. With that truth in mind, we agreed to compromise. Maybe the purchase of a hot dog, a drink, and a pennant was excessive or too expensive. Likewise, absolutely and adamantly refusing all of these purchases might be a little obsessive too. Our compromise was this: At the ballpark, we will buy one thing for each child . . . a hot dog, a drink, a pennant, etc. If someone wants to purchase more than one thing, he may do so with the money that he has earned.

We came to a compromise that both of us could support. We communicated it to the kids. That became the normal for our family. They had seen the conflict before the resolution, and they witnessed the conversation in which the honest communication began. That conversation led to the compromise, the new normal for our family.

Chances are you know exactly what I mean about your normal and the normal of your spouse being different. You can probably list some of the differences between what you brought to your marriage and what your spouse brought in. If you have never considered this before, let me prime the pump for you.

"The River"

As I was preparing to work on this section of the book I found myself in the perfect setting for research. I was not at a university or at a public library. I was at a family reunion along the Tippecanoe River in Indiana.

This family reunion that I have attended for more than thirty-five years is unlike any I had previously encountered or have ever read about. The event, fondly referred to as "The River," has been in existence for more than sixty years and is very well attended. The reunion in its entirety lasts for more than a week. The accommodations for this extended event range from tents to camping trailers to motor homes to hotel reservations in town.

The adults, usually numbering close to fifty, spend the days sitting in lawn chairs around the fire . . . talking and laughing and generally enjoying one another while the kids ride bikes, go on hikes, and tube down the river. Oh yes, and there are raspberries to pick and a big round barn to explore and a volleyball game if you can convince others to play. The drinking and washing water comes from a hand pump and the other facilities are, shall we say, rustic.

To the people who have spent a portion of each year of their life at this reunion, this is normal. Their spouses do not necessarily classify this extended family reunion as normal. I discovered in my research that there was a common reaction by the spouses when asked about how normal they found this week of camping. Most of the respondents knowingly rolled their eyes and smiled. This eye-rolling did not necessarily indicate displeasure with the yearly camping experience; it was simply a response to the use of the word *normal* in conjunction with the words "The River." The families I interviewed all have established their new normal, which includes this reunion each year. Years from now their children will probably marry and have to explain to their spouses why this particular gathering is normal.

More Than Reunions

Traditions can vary well beyond the way a family reunion is celebrated. One of the more common differences that each spouse brings into the marriage has to do with food . . . what is served, how it is served, the quantity served, and the time it is served.

I am the youngest of three kids by several years. The majority of my growing up was spent like an only child. My mother was serious about cooking nutritious, delicious meals every day. This didn't necessarily differ from John's experiences at the dinner table, but one thing was very different. My mother's idea of a successful meal was to cook exactly the right amount of food and end up with no leftovers. John's mom was appalled if there were no leftovers. If that happened, she feared that someone had not gotten enough to eat. Creating a new normal meant deciding whether leftovers were a liability or a bonus.

Foods that are normal and appealing to one spouse may seem very unusual and unappealing to another. The more ethnic the dish, the greater the risk, but even the ingredients in a meatloaf can motivate a discussion about what is normal.

Jane, a friend of mine who was raised in the Midwest, prepared to marry Jerome, a gentleman from Great Britain. She had always wanted a carrot cake for her wedding, which, personally, I deem very normal. She was to discover, however, that in England carrot cake for a wedding was far from normal. Instead she was expected to have fruit cake. (Is that normal?) By Jane's choice, their beautiful English wedding featured fruit cake, a testimony to her love, respect, and willingness to opt for normal as Jerome knew it.

The Holidays

It's difficult to know where to begin when it comes to the differing traditions for the holidays. There will potentially be an exaggerated number of differences in the two "normals" brought to a marriage if you had religious differences. Sometimes spouses find they celebrated different holidays as youngsters. Let's make it much simpler and begin with the premise that you and your spouse both celebrated the same holidays . . . Christmas, New Year's Eve, Easter, Memorial Day, the Fourth of July, Labor Day, and Thanksgiving. If I have failed to list one of your favorites like Groundhog Day, just chalk it up to my thinking that the celebration of that day is not normal.

Maybe your family was very frugal in gift-giving at Christmas.

Maybe they were extravagant. Marrying someone whose normal was not like yours can cause a conflict. As a child, Easter might have been a time for bunnies and colored eggs or entirely a religious celebration. Those differences can cause an upset. Even if it was normal for both you and your spouse to spend Thanksgiving Day at your grandmothers' homes, what happens now that you are married and the grandmothers have multiplied? You will have to decide on your new normal.

Gary's family chose to buy their Christmas tree on Christmas Eve and decorate it that evening. This tradition stemmed in part from the discount price of trees so close to the holiday. Kay's family lived on a farm with a large wooded area. In late November they would hike the woods and cut down the perfect tree. That very fresh fir tree went up in her parents' home right after Thanksgiving and didn't come down until the week after Christmas. Now Gary and Kay were married and they had to decide what would be normal for their family.

Let Me Call You Sweetheart

My parents typically referred to me as "the baby." In fact, my mom introduced me like that to her dying day. I'm sure we confused more than one worker at the nursing home where she lived. My older sister, Patsy, was "Sis," and my brother who shared the same first name as my dad was "Noel-boy"—poor guy. Yet John had learned from his family traditions that nicknames were not normal.

That was not the only disconnect we encountered when it came to addressing another person. Although we used pet names in our home, we referred to people outside our home with great respect. In other words, it was Mr. and Mrs. Wilson, not Marge and Duke; Mrs. Harr, not Erma; Mrs. Jackson, not . . . honestly, I don't even know her first name. John's upbringing taught just the opposite. His preschool Sunday school teacher, who was past sixty-five years old when I met her, had been Zola to him since she had him in her class. That is just not normal!

Some families choose to address one another in a way that expresses their affection. Maybe your mom or dad called each other "Honey" or "Sweetheart," or some other term of endearment. Perhaps directly articulating your love for the people in your home was an everyday thing. The woman who has countless times heard her father tell her mother, "I love you," will expect to hear the same from her husband. There will probably be trouble if his normal had an understood yet unexpressed, "I love you."

Vacations and Recreation

I had never camped before I met my husband. My first camping experience was my first trip to "The River." My family stayed in hotels. We had what some might refer to as more sophisticated experiences. I must admit that I am now a camping convert, enjoying almost every aspect of the experience from the beautiful evening campfires to rushing outside the tent in the middle of the night to put up the rain fly as it begins to sprinkle. (I should probably say cheering on John as he puts the rain fly on our tent.)

Camping is not everyone's cup of tea. My good friend Sue, whom I have tried for years to convince that camping might be fun, has informed me that her idea of roughing it is to fail to make reservations. She would have had a hard time with John's normal. Her husband, Rich, however, did not have camping in his tradition package, so she is fine.

Our children have enjoyed both worlds. They have been on camping trips all of their lives and have also seen the inside of some beautiful hotels. I remember thinking that I wanted our children to know how to find the appropriate stick to roast a hot dog over the fire *and* which fork to use when presented with more than one at an elegant place setting— a taste of both traditions.

Maybe you are a mountain climber or someone who sails. You will be able to continue with those normal recreation endeavors if your spouse either shares your enthusiasm or is willing to adjust.

And the List Goes On

We could go on and on when it comes to areas where your "normals" might differ.

Some families live by the motto, "Early to bed and early to rise . . ." Some prefer to burn the midnight oil and then sleep in. When the kids arrive you will have to identify what works for your family.

One family very seldom visits the physician. Another goes for every ache and pain. The decision will have to be made about what is best when there is an ailing child.

Scott has no qualms about stopping in to visit a neighbor. His wife, Kolene, considers dropping in on someone rude, and she certainly doesn't want their children to be rude!

Debbie rolled her sweet corn in the butter from the butter dish. Jim put butter on his corn with a knife. It really did not matter until it came time to see that the kids did it right.

Nathan's family set out the kids' toys unwrapped at Christmas. Leah's mom always wrapped everything. Would their kids tear into the wrapping paper or wonder why others ever used it?

Brian's family ate dinner at 6:00 p.m. Shelby's ate when it was ready . . . eventually. At her parents' home Brian put up with the hassle of waiting . . . until the kids arrived. Then he wanted things to be normal.

Patti and her folks only went to church occasionally. Kevin's family was there every time the doors were open. Patti and Kevin needed to decide how they would operate in their home.

I Did It My Way

If either you or your spouse is not willing to dialogue and compromise in the area of family traditions, problems can arise. I know of a man who, as an adult, told his parents that he intended to raise his children exactly the way he had been raised. This does not leave room for (a) improvement or (b) input from his wife. Although that might sound like a compliment to his parents, it is actually an admission of the intent to do it *his* way. Whether that refers to child rearing in general or specifically to family traditions, that declaration is not the best.

I used to say with a humorous tone, "I am not going to make *any* of the mistakes my parents made. That will give me more time for mistakes of my own." Did I repeat their mistakes? Sure, some of them. Did I make any of my own? Absolutely. But I believe I learned to dialogue, negotiate, and compromise. John and I chose to blend our "normals," our traditions. When you love your spouse in that way, you are doing your kids a favor.

Our kids learned that doing things *exactly* like we did was not the answer for them as adults. They learned that someday they would have the opportunity to create a new normal for their own family and that the task would take compromise. They would be able to choose to do their kids a favor and love their spouses.

A Good Word from John, the Resident Dad

Most of us think of our traditions as something positive. However, when two people with different "normals" marry, they might discover that their traditions collide and cause a problem. That is when the opportunity arises to work together and establish a new normal for your family. You do not have to wait for a conflict, however, to create a new tradition. Two of my favorite family traditions were originals that we created.

The First Tradition

At Christmastime for more than twenty years the five of us made yeast donuts. We gave them as gifts to family and friends. Kendra and I would get up very early and stir up the dough. Then we waited for the dough (and our boys) to rise. After a few hours the five of us were hard at work—cutting donuts, letting them rise again, deep fat frying, and frosting them. Oh, and did I mention eating donuts and donut holes until we were almost too full to finish the job?

After the donuts were put on Christmas trays, we all piled into the car for the deliveries. Our kids had definitely lost some of their enthusiasm by then, but each carried a tray up to the two homes of the families he had personally chosen for that year.

The day was fun for each of us. More important, giving to others of our time and talents in the shape of a donut became the normal thing to do.

The Second Tradition

The second tradition continues to this day and it is the most meaningful for me. It also occurs during the Christmas season.

Before we open our gifts to one another we go around the room and each family member tells one thing he or she has learned from the Lord during the past year. Kendra and I participate, as do our sons and now their wives. This time together is powerful and poignant, and it directs our thoughts to our relationships with one another and with our Lord.

Do not miss the opportunity to introduce a new tradition to your family, to try something that is original and different. The only caution is to be certain that the tradition honors God. This was the challenge that Jesus brought to the Pharisees.

> Then some Pharisees and teachers of the law came to Jesus from Jerusalem and asked, "Why do your disciples break the tradition of the elders? They don't wash their hands before they eat!"
>
> Jesus replied, "And why do you break the command of God for the sake of your tradition? For God said, 'Honor your father and mother' and 'Anyone who curses his father or mother must be put to death.' But you say that if a man says to his father or mother, 'Whatever help you might otherwise have received from me is a gift devoted to God,' he is not to 'honor his father' with it. Thus you nullify the word of God for the sake of your tradition. You hypocrites! Isaiah was right when he prophesied about you: 'These people honor me with their lips, but their hearts are far from me. They worship me in vain; their teachings are but rules taught by men.'" (Matt. 15:1–9)

Many of the actions and decisions of Jesus challenged the traditions of His day. These challenges were made when those traditions were in conflict with what God had commanded. The truth of the Word was Christ's benchmark. That should be the plumb line for us too.

Most traditions are neither right nor wrong. The "normals" that we bring into a family are usually just different. But if those traditions happen to contradict the truth of God, it is time to make a change. And when you establish a new normal, be certain that it glorifies God. That is one way to do your kids a favor.

Last, but Not Least

You will want to examine one last subject in order to do your kids a favor and love your spouse—identity theft. You might wonder what that topic has to do with you as a spouse and a parent. With identity theft an increasing concern in our nation, we will take a look at how you can protect your true identity, and, more important, how you can establish a positive identity model for your kids.

Time for Some Honest Reflection

1. Think of a situation in which your spouse has chosen to adapt to your normal. Thank him or her for being wonderfully flexible and sweet.

2. What is a tradition from your family of origin that your spouse would question as normal? Now it is your turn. What tradition did your spouse's family have that you are *sure* was not normal?

3. Name one example of when you and your spouse have chosen a "new normal" for your own family. Ask your spouse to think of another one.

4. Now think of an issue where your "normals" are still colliding. Propose a time when you and your spouse can discuss this issue unemotionally. When you have agreed on a time, put it on the calendar and move toward establishing a new normal.

5. Are you being stubborn and failing to embrace a tradition that your spouse feels is important? If so, step back and reconsider. Maybe you need to be more flexible. You might be missing a great new family tradition.

CHAPTER SIX

Identity Theft: Can Someone Really Steal It?

"I'm sorry, Kendra," said Josh, the owner of the flower shop. "For some reason your credit card won't clear."

"I can't imagine why. It couldn't be that I'm over my limit. If that's the case," I said, smiling, "I'm in big trouble."

How embarrassing! Thank goodness I was at a store in a small town where the owner is my friend. He probably would have let me take my purchases home and mail him a check, but I reached into my wallet and gave him a different card.

"I'll give the credit card company a call when I get home. Thanks!"

I cut my errands short and went home to call.

"Yes, Mrs. Smiley, I'm looking at your account now. We put a hold on your number this morning because of a suspicious charge. Did you order a collection of G.I. Joe dolls and accessories over the Internet totaling $936.85?" she inquired calmly.

With that question my calm was gone! "Absolutely not! I didn't even spend $9.85 on G.I. Joes. I haven't made a G.I. Joe purchase in years!"

"No problem," she replied. "That expenditure was denied because we suspected it wasn't yours. That's why your credit card number was placed on hold."

"Does that mean someone has stolen my identity?" I asked,

hyperventilating as I remembered the last news special I saw about the perils of identity theft.

"No ma'am. Someone stole your credit card number, not your identity. It will be an inconvenience to you, but it's not nearly as serious as identity theft. You will not be charged for purchases you did not make, and we will issue you a new number today. Please stay on the line so I can get some information from you."

What a relief! Inconvenience I can deal with. Identity theft would have been awful!

New Numbers

It took me several days to receive my new credit card number and to contact all the companies and organizations that charged directly to my account. During that time I began to consider the whole concept of identity theft.

Could someone actually steal my identity? Can it be taken away from me? I know firsthand that my credit card number can be stolen. And I have heard of people's social security numbers and driver's license numbers being illegally used by others. But I question the idea that a collection of numbers constitutes someone's identity. We are more than identifying digits.

John's Story

I was not necessarily the victim of identity theft. For me it was more like looking in the spot where I thought I had put my identity, and realizing it was not there.

I accepted Christ as my Savior when I was sixteen years old, and to the best of my ability began to pursue the truth. Since that time I graduated from high school and college, taught school, worked as an independent sales representative, flew jets for the Air Force and Air Force Reserves, and farmed 680 acres of corn and soybeans. For most of those years, I did not think very much about my identity, nor did I look too closely at what Jesus might be saying in Matthew 6:21, "For where your treasure is, there your heart will be also."

Then in February 2002, after thirty years of service, my days as an Air Force officer and jet pilot came to a close. It was the end of my career with the United States Air Force Reserves. When you retire from the Reserves, you are not entitled to retirement pay until you reach the age of sixty. I was fifty-two. At that point I looked for a civilian flying position . . . unsuccessfully.

Kendra and I were able to pay our bills, but something major had changed. I had lost my joy. I was depressed and started searching, asking God, "What am I supposed to do now?" I never heard or sensed an answer to that question. Surely God wanted me to *do* something. I had always *done* something. I had been a working man since my grade-school days.

My Treasure

Instead of hearing from God about my next job, it seemed as though He wanted me to focus on the location of my treasure, my identity. What was it again that Jesus said about a man's treasure?

> "Do not store up for yourselves treasures on earth, where moth and rust destroy, and where thieves break in and steal. But store up for yourselves treasures in heaven, where moth and rust do not destroy, and where thieves do not break in and steal. For where your treasure is, there your heart will be also." (Matt. 6:19–21)

I was certain that my treasure was in Jesus. But if it was, why was I out of sorts and depressed? He had not changed just because I was no longer flying jets. Maybe my identity was not where I thought it was.

I kept searching and asking God to show me the truth. And He did. Even though I had been a Christian since my teenage years, and had tried to follow Him in my life, I came to realize that my treasure did not lie in Him. My treasure was in making money. My identity was in my ability to produce an income that was more than adequate. My treasure wasn't in hoarding money or spending it on myself, but my joy came from being able to earn a good salary. It was fun to make money, and flying jets was the means to that end. Now that door had been closed, slammed shut because of my number of years of service. I found myself missing my poorly placed treasure. In a sense, my identity was gone. God did not want to direct me to a new job to answer the question, "What do You want me to do now?" He wanted me to take a long, hard look at the location of my treasure.

Changing Focus

As I came to the truth about my misplaced treasure, I knew I had to change my focus. My identity was not to be in something as shallow as making money. It was to be in my heavenly Father.

I would love to tell you that this realization had enough impact to change my depressed attitude and give me joy in the true treasure. I would love to tell you that, but it wouldn't be the truth. No, just realizing that my identity was not in Christ was not enough. I have had to struggle with that truth. I have spent long hours praying and reading and talking with fellow Christians, especially with Kendra. All that has helped me move toward the true treasure, the treasure found in Christ.

What Does That Look Like?

When I discovered that my identity was not where it should be, I searched for an illustration of what I was now pursuing. I wanted to see what having one's identity in Jesus might look like.

For me, that example came in the person of Eric Liddell, the Olympic runner from Scotland. Perhaps you know his story. It was immortalized in the movie *Chariots of Fire*. In a nutshell, Eric was a Christian bound for the mission field. He was also an outstanding runner, and he became a contestant and representative of his country in the 1924 Olympics. His sister confronted him about his running, fearing that it had become his identity, replacing Christ. His reply honored God for making him fast, and he added, "and when I run, I feel His pleasure." In essence, he was not running and competing to replace God; he was running to please God. He was a Christian who ran, not a runner who happened to be a Christian.

His commitment to Christ was vividly illustrated when he qualified for the Olympic finals in the 100 meter dash, his best race. It was, however, to be run on Sunday, and Eric Liddell withdrew because of that fact. He found himself under intense pressure from his teammates and delegates from his homeland, but he held his ground. In his eyes, running on Sunday would not glorify God. He was a Christian who ran, not a runner who happened to be a Christian. Liddell went on to win an Olympic gold medal in another race later that week.

The point is not whether you choose to run or not to run on Sunday. The point is: Where is your identity—your primary identity? For myself, I had to ask, Was I a Christian pilot or a pilot who happened to be a Christian? Was I a Christian wage earner or a wage earner who happened to be a Christian?

Living Illustration

I had searched to find a picture of someone whose identity was in Christ. Now that became my personal pursuit—to be that example and picture for my family. I needed to be a living illustration for Kendra and for our kids. The question now became: What does that look like in *my* life?

By the time this became my goal, I was no longer flying for a living. Instead I was farming, raising corn and soybeans. That was a very big career change even though agriculture had been a part of my civilian life when I was in the Reserves

When you are a crop farmer there are several weeks every spring and fall that are incredibly important. Obviously, they are the time when the crop is planted and when it is harvested. Those days of working can be twelve to sixteen hours long and the labor is physically taxing.

One of the first spring seasons after my resolve to put my

identity in Christ, I was in the midst of that busy time. I received a phone call from an acquaintance who lived on the East Coast. He was in Illinois, about three hours from our home, and wondered if I could meet him for lunch somewhere. He wanted to talk with me. He had no idea that he was making this request during one of the busiest and most critical weeks of the farming year. All he knew was that he needed to talk with me and he was closer than he had ever been to our farm.

What was I supposed to do? The answer could only come from God. I committed my friend's request to prayer and listened for God's answer. Ultimately, I agreed to a meeting. The next day I climbed off my tractor, took a quick shower, and met him for lunch.

Now being a Christian who happens to be a farmer doesn't mean that I would always take a day off farming when someone wants to meet for lunch. Stopping in the middle of the workday even to minister to someone isn't a sign that your identity is properly placed. Just as in the example of Eric Liddell, the point is not whether you choose to run or not to run on Sunday. The point is: Where is your identity—your primary identity? Was I a Christian farmer or a farmer who happened to be a Christian? I had to be willing to try to discern what the Lord would have me do in that particular situation.

A few months later, in the busy fall season of farming, a similar situation arose. Interestingly, as Kendra and I prayed about what I should do, we both felt that the answer that time was not to take the day off, so I declined the invitation. Following Christ is a continual process permeated with the desire to have my identity where it should be.

The Favor

The process of truly placing your identity in Christ will have an impact on both your spouse and your kids.

Our children will see the truth that no matter what may seem more exciting or important or tantalizing, putting their identity in Jesus is the best choice when we, as parents, place our identity in Him. When our treasure is where it should be, we are loving our family and doing our kids a favor, in this case one very important favor.

Consequences

You might think that since my treasure was misplaced for several years I was consumed with being busy and making money. That was not the case. Marriage takes time and I was committed to giving that time to our marriage and to our family. Being a godly dad meant that I needed to be present with the boys. I knew these things and I turned down many opportunities to make *more* money in order to be home with my family. I could have pursued a civilian flying job while in the Reserves and added that to my résumé and my income. Even though I avoided that pitfall, there were still consequences for having my focus on the wrong treasure. One, in particular, was friction between Kendra and me.

After Jonathan, our youngest son, started elementary school, I wanted Kendra to return to her profession of teaching. I knew that it would be much more lucrative than what she felt God was calling her to do. My goal was for her to make more money. I was upset she would not see it my way. When I finally realized that she would not change her mind, it seemed that my best choice would be to support her decision and encourage her. After all, maybe she could make even more money in direct sales, and then in speaking and writing, than she could teaching school. Even though she rose to be a top performer in the direct sales company she represented and had numerous speaking engagements each year, she never came close to making as much as she would have teaching school with her advanced degree. My secret plan was not working.

False Assumption

During those years I was not truthful with myself. I assumed that God was the treasure of my life, but that was not the case. Through all those years my three sons were watching. They knew I loved the Lord, but something was not quite right. My theory was that being a Christian made me the best pilot possible. That would have been true if my treasure had been in Christ. But I was a pilot who just happened to be a Christian. My primary identity was in what I was doing and the earthly rewards that it brought. "Where your treasure is," Jesus said, "there will your heart be also."

My heart finally began to change. My desire became to have my treasure, my identity, in Jesus. I wish I had learned this lesson earlier so that the favor would have been more powerful for all of my kids. But I am thankful that God revealed His truth to me. Where is your identity? Where is your treasure? Put it in Christ. That will help you love your spouse and do your kids a favor.

A Mother's Story

It is very possible that you, as a mom, can relate wholeheartedly to John's story. Perhaps your career and the joys and challenges it presents have become your identity. You may be a physician who happens to be a Christian. Or a teacher who happens to be a Christian. Or a CEO who happens to be a Christian. Or a real estate agent who happens to be a Christian. Or a _____ who happens to be a Christian. (Please fill in the blank.) Stop and evaluate whether or not your career or profession is your primary identity.

It is also possible that you cannot imagine your job being that important. But you can see it would be easy to let being a mom become your identity. Or your identity comes from being a wife.

In my growing up years, when people asked me what I wanted to be when I grew up I always answered, "A teacher." And a teacher is what I became. I loved teaching school. I loved the kids and the fun of watching them learn. I loved the socialization with my colleagues. There was very little I didn't like. But somehow the answer to that question from my youth began to change. After teaching for several years, if someone had asked me, "What do you want to be when you grow up?" I would have said, "I want to be a mom."

And that is precisely what happened. When John and I discovered that we had a baby on the way, I was thrilled. I was a mom. A year or so after Matthew was born I began working from my home, writing and speaking, and blending that with motherhood. At that point I actually had to look at two important issues. Was I a mom who happened to be a Christian? Or a Christian who was a mom? Was I a speaker and writer who happened to be a Christian? Or a Christian who was a speaker and writer? It was important for John to identify where his treasure was, and it was equally important for me.

Follow the Leader

I wanted John to share his story first because it was his struggle and eventual triumph that led me to take a close look at my identity. Just like John, my identity was not in a series of digits like my credit card number or my social security number. Beyond that similarity, however, my experience did not completely parallel his. The satisfaction I received from my job, speaking and writing, did not have the same impact on me as his flying position did on him.

That is not to insinuate that women do not struggle to keep their vocations from dominating their identity, but because we are so adept at multitasking, we seem to be capable of allowing many things to simultaneously become our misplaced identities. It can be motherhood, careers, hobbies, income, marriage, titles, and/or social status. The list is disgustingly long and the combinations are endless.

For me the combination was motherhood, career, and fun. That last one didn't even make my list above because I am aware that it sounds trivial and insignificant. But I know it will make sense to you when you reflect on the chapter on the differing personalities. I am a social being —an extrovert who loves people. I enjoy my career *and* I like being a mom. At any given time, I might find my identity misplaced in one of those three categories. I can be a people-lover who happens to be a Christian. I can be an author who happens to be a Christian. I can be a mom who happens to be a Christian. Or I can make the best choice to be a Christian who is a loving extrovert, a speaker and writer, and a mom.

You might need to add the question: Are you a wife who happens to be a Christian or a Christian who is a wife? Some women find their identity in their relationship to their husbands.

My actions and decisions will give me away. If the party is more important than Jesus, I've misplaced my identity. If the speaking engagement or the book deadline is more important than Jesus, I've misplaced my identity. If my children are more important than Jesus, I have misplaced my identity. Can anyone steal my identity? No, not my true identity. But I can certainly misplace it. I will only know by being honest with myself. God already knows.

It is a daily, sometimes hourly, choice for me—the choice of where to put my identity. I don't always choose wisely. But even when I have misplaced my identity once again, I realize that my responsibility is simply to make the next right choice and get back on track. If I make the next right choice and follow that with the next right choice and follow that with the next right choice, I am closer to keeping my identity where it should be—in Christ. I am closer to being a living illustration for my family. I am loving my husband and doing my kids a favor.

A Good Word from John, the Resident Dad

Following the crucifixion of Christ, the disciples were upset, confused, and probably a little scared. What were they supposed to do now? Simon Peter had been a fisherman. He chose to go back to the sea—a place where he was comfortable —a place that had been a part of his identity for years. Peter chose to go fishing. Join me and read the words of John 21:4–15.

> Early in the morning, Jesus stood on the shore, but the disciples did not realize that it was Jesus.
> He called out to them, "Friends, haven't you any fish?"
> "No," they answered.
> He said, "Throw your net on the right side of the boat and you will find some." When they did, they were unable to haul the net in because of the large number of fish.

Peter, the spontaneous, passionate disciple, threw himself into the water to swim to Jesus. Jesus fed His disciples, and then

He looked at the one who had recently betrayed Him, and asked the same question three times.

> When they had finished eating, Jesus said to Simon Peter, "Simon son of John, do you truly love me more than these?"

> "Yes, Lord," he said, "you know that I love you."
> Jesus said, "Feed my lambs."

Peter must have been confused when Jesus questioned him more than once, "Do you love me more than these?" These? What did Jesus mean when He asked Peter if he loved Him "more than these"?

The fish—it was the fish! Jesus wanted to know what Peter loved more . . . Him or the fish. Was Peter's identity once again in being a fisherman? Was he a Christian who was a fisherman? Or a fisherman who happened to be a Christian? Those two questions, in one form or another, are the ones each of us must consider. We must determine if our identity lies in Christ or in something or someone else.

Time for Some Honest Reflection

1. If you have misplaced your identity, where is it likely to be found?

2. Where would your spouse find his or her misplaced identity?

3. Fill in the blank. Am I a Christian _____? Or a _____ who happens to be a Christian? How would you answer these questions?

4. How did you determine your answers? What actions and decisions gave you away?

5. Jesus asked, "Do you love me more than *these*?" (my italics) What is your "these"? What is your answer?

The Fifteen-Year Plan

John and I say, reluctantly, that we were on the fifteen-year plan. According to our estimation, it took us close to fifteen years to come to realize the importance of the things we have just shared with you.

During those fifteen years we began to work toward an understanding of our gender differences. We came to the realization that our personalities were very different, and, more important, that we appreciated each other's strengths. The unpacking process began as layers of baggage were uncovered, with more yet to come. We evaluated the different "normals" we each brought into our marriage and created a new normal for our family. And finally, more recently, we faced the reality that our identities needed to be in the true treasure, in Christ.

Some of those things were easier than others. Wait. Let me reword that. None of those things was easy. Some were less difficult. It has been my experience that introspection is not an easy thing to do. It is unpleasant and arduous and disagreeable and far from amusing. But that really does not matter, if you keep your goal in mind. That goal is to do your kids a favor and love your spouse. Success will not be instantaneous or complete, but the idea is to move forward in the process.

I read a statement several years ago that has become one of my "quotable quotes." Originally, I deemed it the definition of an adult. My version goes like this: An adult is someone who does what needs to be done . . . *when* it needs to be done . . . whether he wants to do it or not.

Since my initial declaration of this statement describing an adult, I have decided it also is the definition of success. Success is doing what needs to be done . . . *when* it needs to be done . . . whether you want to do it or not.

So as an adult who wants to be a success as a spouse and as a parent, it is time to get going. Fifteen years is much too long! I do not want our sons and their wives to subscribe to that extended plan. I do not want you to wait that long either. Hence, the book you hold in your hands.

I truly believe that the Lord can dramatically shorten your learning curve and that you can trim years off the fifteen-year plan by profiting from our experiences. If you are already beyond the fifteen-year mark, do not dismay. Instead commit these words of Scripture to memory: "I will repay you for the years the locusts have eaten" (Joel 2:25).

Do your kids a favor. Love your spouse!

God's Plan of Salvation

The Bible Says There Is Only One Way to Have a Right Relationship with God.

Jesus answered: "I am the way and the truth and the life. No one comes to the Father except through me." (John 14:6)

For all have sinned and fall short of the glory of God. (Romans 3:23)

Therefore, just as sin entered the world through one man, and death through sin, and in this way death came to all men, because all sinned. (Romans 5:12)

But God demonstrates his own love for us in this: While we were still sinners, Christ died for us. (Romans 5:8)

That if you confess with your mouth, "Jesus is Lord," and believe in your heart that God raised him from the dead, you will be saved. (Romans 10:9)

For it is with your heart that you believe and are justified, and it is with your mouth that you confess and are saved. (Romans 10:10)

Everyone who calls on the name of the Lord will be saved. (Romans 10:13)

What to Pray

Dear God, I am a sinner and need forgiveness. I believe that Jesus Christ shed His precious blood and died for my sin. I am willing to turn from sin. I now invite Christ to come into my heart and life as my personal Savior.

After you make your decision to follow Christ, it is important to get involved in a Bible-believing church. Read and study the Bible. (The gospel of John is a great place to start.) Begin a prayer life with God.

Acknowledgments

We had the privilege of working on this book with the help of several special people. Our thanks go to Elizabeth Newenhuyse, Moody Publishers editorial director, whose encouragement, guidance, and vision were a blessing.

One of the joys of doing a book project with Moody Publishers is the anticipation of working with Janis Backing, our publicist. Janis brings professionalism and enthusiasm to her role and consistently demonstrates Christian commitment and excellence. Anyone in the industry knows she is one of the best.

Thanks to Kevin Howells, our manager, who is a creative guy! His outstanding input teamed with his impeccable integrity are a gift to us.

One of the goals in parenting is to work your way out of a job. Hands-on parenting usually lasts for only eighteen years, and then you move into the role of consultant and friend. We are blessed to be in that second stage with our three sons and their wives. Thank you Matthew and Marissa, Aaron and Kristin, and Jonathan and Ashley for your love, humor, and encouragement.

Our "forever thanks" go to the Lord. We pray that this book will bring glory to Him and encourage and equip you, the reader, to *Do Your Kids a Favor . . . Love Your Spouse.*

Kendra and John Smiley

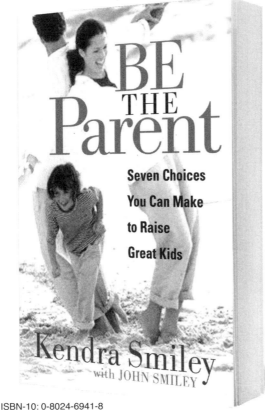

BE THE Parent

Seven Choices You Can Make to Raise Great Kids

Kendra Smiley
with JOHN SMILEY

ISBN-10: 0-8024-6941-8
ISBN-13: 978-0-8024-6941-0

Kendra Smiley, author of *Aaron's Way* and *Do Your Kids a Favor* once again hits on a subject that moms and dads are longing to hear–how can I be a better parent and raise great and godly children? With wisdom gleaned both as parent and teacher, Kendra suggests seven proactive choices parents can make to help reduce family stress and avoid parenting emergencies. Each chapter ends with a dash of advice from her husband, John, who offers a dad's point of view. Whether exhausted and struggling or just longing to improve their skills, *Be the Parent* is the perfect resource for moms and dads seeking to positively impact their children. Includes survey responses from real parents.

by Kendra Smiley
Find it now at your favorite local or online bookstore.

www.MoodyPublishers.com

ED YOUNG

ED YOUNG
Foreword by Beth Moore

THE **10** COMMANDMENTS OF
parenting

THE **10** COMMANDMENTS OF
marriage

The Do's and Don'ts for Raising Great Kids

The Do's and Don'ts for a Lifelong Covenant

ISBN-10: 0-8024-3148-8
ISBN-13: 978-0-8024-3148-6

ISBN-10: 0-8024-3145-3
ISBN-13: 978-0-8024-3145-5

New moms and dads always have the same reaction: "I had no idea it would be this hard!" But you can make it a little easier—and a lot more rewarding—simply by following *The 10 Commandments of Parenting*.

In words that are profound, often humorous, but always biblical, Ed Young draws from decades of counseling couples to provide ten commandments for a lifelong marriage that sizzles. God wants your marriage to be nothing short of incredible.

by Ed Young
Find it now at your favorite local or online bookstore.

www.MoodyPublishers.com

Keep up to date with Kendra online

Live life intentionally!

Teaching people how to make the next right choice

www.KendraSmiley.com